Colby College
Waterville, Maine

Written by Allyson Rudolph
Edited by Kevin Nash

Additional contributions by Omid Gohari,
Christina Koshzow, Chris Mason, Jesse Merkelson, Joey Rahimi,
Jon Skindzier, Luke Skurman, Tim Williams,
Kimberly Moore and Kristen Burns

ISBN # 1-59658-027-5
ISSN # 1551-9724

Special thanks to Babs Carryer, Andy Hannah, LaunchCyte, Tim O'Brien, Bob Sehlinger, Thomas Emerson, Andrew Skurman, Barbara Skurman, Bert Mann, Dave Lehman, Daniel Fayock, Chris Babyak, The Donald H. Jones Center for Entrepreneurship, Terry Slease, Jerry McGinnis, Bill Ecenberger, Idie McGinty, Kyle Russell, Jacque Zaremba, Larry Winderbaum, Paul Kelly, Roland Allen, Jon Reider, Team Evankovich, Julie Fenstermaker, Lauren Varacalli, Abu Noaman, Jason Putorti, Mark Exler, Daniel Steinmeyer, Jared Cohon, Gabriela Oates, Tri Ad Litho, David Koegler, Glen Meakem, and the Colby College Bounce Back Team.

College Prowler™
5001 Baum Blvd.
Suite 456
Pittsburgh, PA 15213

Phone: (412) 697-1390, 1(800) 290-2682
Fax: (412) 697-1396, 1(800) 772-4972
E-mail: info@collegeprowler.com
Website: www.collegeprowler.com

Welcome to College Prowler™

During the writing of College Prowler's guidebooks, we felt it was critical that our content was unbiased and unaffiliated with any college or university. We think it's important that our readers get honest information and a realistic impression of the student opinions on any campus — that's why if any aspect of a particular school is terrible, we (unlike a campus brochure) intend to publish it. While we do keep an eye out for the occasional extremist — the cheerleader or the cynic — we take pride in letting the students tell it like it is. We strive to create a book that's as representative as possible of each particular campus. Our books cover both the good and the bad, and whether the survey responses point to recurring trends or a variation in opinion, these sentiments are directly and proportionally expressed through our guides.

College Prowler guidebooks are in the hands of students throughout the entire process of their creation. Because you can't make student-written guides without the students, we have students at each campus who help write, randomly survey their peers, edit, layout, and perform accuracy checks on every book that we publish. From the very beginning, student writers gather the most up-to-date stats, facts, and inside information on their colleges. They fill each section with student quotes and summarize the findings in editorial reviews. In addition, each school receives a collection of letter grades (A through F) that reflect student opinion and help to represent contentment, prominence, or satisfaction for each of our 20 specific categories. Just as in grade school, the higher the mark the more content, more prominent, or more satisfied the students are with the particular category.

Once a book is written, additional students serve as editors and check for accuracy even more extensively. Our bounce-back team — a group of randomly selected students who have no involvement with the project — are asked to read over the material in order to help ensure that the book accurately expresses every aspect of the university and its students. This same process is applied to the 200-plus schools College Prowler currently covers. Each book is the result of endless student contributions, hundreds of pages of research and writing, and countless hours of hard work. All of this has led to the creation of a student information network that stretches across the nation to every school that we cover. It's no easy accomplishment, but it's the reason that our guides are such a great resource.

When reading our books and looking at our grades, keep in mind that every college is different and that the students who make up each school are not uniform — as a result, it is important to assess schools on a case-by-case basis. Because it's impossible to summarize an entire school with a single number or description, each book provides a dialogue, not a decision, that's made up of 20 different topics and hundreds of student quotes. In the end, we hope that this guide will serve as a valuable tool in your college selection process. Enjoy!

OMID GOHARI ○ CHRISTINA KOSHZOW ○ CHRIS MASON ○ JOEY RAHIMI ○ LUKE SKURMAN ○
The College Prowler™ Team

Table of Contents

Introduction from the Author

Colby College is the kind of small New England liberal arts school
that's well known and well reputed—as long as you're talking to
someone else who went to a small New England liberal arts school.
If you're from the Midwest, people will think you're going to a school
named for cheese, and make never-ending dairy product jokes.
For those who are curious, the school is named for Gardiner Colby,
a wealthy man who saved the school when all its students started
getting drafted away to the Civil War—not cheese. Colby is one of
many liberal arts schools that most high school students discover
for the first time during their college search. On paper, Colby looks
almost identical to many of its neighbors. The school is known for its
strong academics, its small classes, and its bucolic beauty.

At Colby it's perfectly okay to be undecided on your major, your
career goal, and even your classes for next semester. It's pretty normal
to be a biology major one day and a theatre major the next, or even
both at once. Don't get worried, though, Colby students aren't
clueless. Typically we're just really interested in a vast number of
subjects. But this, too, is typical of New England liberal arts schools.

So what sets Colby apart? It's hard to quantify the subtle differences
that influence a person's choice in colleges. The best bet, of course, is
to visit the school, and to read this book (Oh, come on, you knew that
was coming, right?).

Most people will tell you that they came to Colby for the people. The
academics are stellar, but the friendly students and easy-to-talk-to
faculty and administration have hooked more prospective freshmen
than anything else. No matter how cold the winters get, and no
matter how far you have to drive to go shopping somewhere other
than Wal-Mart, the students are optimistic and easy-going.

This book offers lots of numbers and facts. It also offers real-live
student opinions. There are funny responses, serious thoughts, insider
advice, and even a couple of secrets. This book has the numbers and
has the facts, but it also tries to include the personalities of Colby's
unique student body. Hopefully you will find it helpful, and good luck
with your college search!

Allyson Rudolph, Author
Colby College

By the Numbers

General Information

Colby College
4000 Mayflower Hill Drive
Waterville, Maine 04901

Control:
Private

Academic Calendar:
4-1-4

Religious Affiliation:
None

Founded:
1813

Website:
www.colby.edu

Main Phone:
(207) 872-3000

Admissions Phone:
(207) 872-3474

Student Body

**Full-Time
Undergraduates:**
1,768

**Part-Time
Undergraduates:**
0

**Full-Time Male
Undergraduates:**
817

**Full-Time Female
Undergraduates:**
951

Male to Female Ratio:
46.2% to 53.8%

Admissions

Overall Acceptance Rate:
34%

Early Decision Acceptance Rate:
40%

Regular Acceptance Rate:
33%

Total Applicants:
4,126

Total Acceptances:
1,388

Freshman Enrollment:
474

Yield (% of admitted students who actually enroll):
34%

Applicants Placed on Waiting List:
651

Applicants Accepted From Waiting List:
322

Students Enrolled From Waiting List:
6

Transfer Applications Received:
128

Transfer Applications Accepted:
22

Transfer Students Enrolled:
7

Transfer Applicant Acceptance Rate:
17%

Early Decision Available?
Yes

Early Action Available?
No

Early Decision Deadline:
November 15

Early Decision Notification:
December 15

Regular Decision Deadline:
January 1

Regular Decision Notification:
April 1

Must-Reply-By Date:
May 1

Common Application Accepted?
Yes

Supplemental Forms?
Yes

Admissions Phone:
1-800-723-3032

Admissions E-mail:
admissions@colby.edu

Admissions Website:
www.colby.edu/admissions

SAT I or ACT Required?
Either

SAT II Requirements
none

**SAT I Range
(25th – 75th Percentile):**
1270-1420

**SAT I Verbal Range
(25th – 75th Percentile):**
 630-710

**SAT I Math Range
(25th – 75th Percentile):**
640-710

Retention Rate:
93%

**Top 10% of
High School Class:**
62%

Application Fee:
$55

Financial Information

Full-Time Tuition:
$39,800

Part-Time Tuition:
None

$40 registration fee
per semester

Room and Board:
included in tuition

Books and Supplies for class:
$1,400

**Average Need-Based
Financial Aid Package:**
$24,111
(including loans, work-study,
grants, and other sources)

**Students Who
Applied For Financial Aid:**
46%

Students Who Received Aid:
40%

Financial Aid Forms Deadline:
February 1

Financial Aid Phone:
(207) 872-3168

Financial Aid E-mail:
admissions@colby.edu

Financial Aid Website:
www.colby.edu/admissions

Academics

The Lowdown On...
Academics

Degrees Awarded:
Bachelor

Most Popular Majors:
13% English literature (British and Commonwealth)
13% biology/biological sciences
13% economics
10% political science and government
8% history

Full-Time Faculty:
158

Faculty with Terminal Degree:
95%

Student-to-Faculty Ratio:
11:1

Average Course Load:
Four

Four Year Graduation Rate
84%

Six Year Graduation Rate
86%

Five Year Graduation Rate
86%

Special Degree Options
None

AP Test Score Requirements
Possible credit for scores of 4 or 5

IB Test Score Requirements
Possible credit for scores of 5,6 or 7

Best Places to Study

Library, Pugh Center, Mary Low Coffeehouse, Spa

Sample Academic Clubs

Computer Club, Debate Team, Student Women in Science, Psychology, Biology (Raging Species), Chemistry, Economics, Geology, Philosophy

Students Speak Out On...
Academics

"In four years I don't think I've had one professor who didn't really care, not only about the class and the material they were teaching, but about me as a student and as a person. Professors are generally wonderful with office hours, and it is not uncommon to be given their house and cell phone numbers as ways to get in touch. Many host class dinners at their houses."

Q "Generally, courses are as interesting as you make them. **Students have so much liberty to choose their own classes**. It would be ridiculous to take a class that you didn't find interesting."

Q **"The teachers are terrific and always willing to help outside of class**. They encourage you to ask for help whenever needed. The classes I took as a freshman were mostly introductory courses, and from what I hear, are not nearly as interesting as the upper-level courses. I still enjoyed them, and am looking forward to more advanced classes."

Q **"My professors were really helpful and engaging**. I believe they truly cared about each individual student, and each student's progress and understanding. I certainly found all of my classes very interesting. I definitely feel refreshed now that I reflect on the classes that I took this year."

Q "The professors are generally really great; some of them are phenomenal. **Some classes at Colby are irreplaceable**. You have to take them because they're that powerful. Of course, there are a couple of standard classes with standard professors, too."

"The **professors at Colby, in general, are extremely knowledgeable, approachable, reputable, and honest**. Many of them are involved in other aspects of student life and classes, and for the most part, are interesting. Of course, you always have a class or two that you don't like, but no school is perfect. On the whole, Colby has an excellent staff of professors."

"**I have been impressed with all of my professors so far.** They all seemed genuinely interested in me, which is impressive considering how many students they have, and how many other things they have to do with their time."

"Teachers are all different of course, but all of them are highly qualified. **Some teachers are super-organized, and others are scattered**. I've never had one that I hated too much. Classes are interesting depending on how much you like the subject. I hate math, but when I took 'Math as a Liberal Art,' I still found myself interested in much of the subject matter. There are plenty of options for requirements so it shouldn't be hard to find something to fit your likes and dislikes."

"**For the most part, the teachers are fantastic**. When working on a paper for government class, my professor always emailed me articles he knew would help my research. In another instance, my French professor asked me to stop by his office after class. It wasn't because I was having trouble with the assignments, but he saw that I was sad and was wondering if I was all right. I love that the teachers are so accessible, and really care about their students."

"**The professors are always willing to help out students**. Yes, some of them might be a little boring or a little weird, but they are nice people once you make the effort to get to know them. Small classes are generally more interesting than the big lectures since more discussion take place between the students and the professor."

Q "Teachers at Colby are incredible. They always find the extra, out of class time to meet with you, and help you until you feel completely comfortable with the material. **I find my classes interesting, especially the ones I'm choosing to take for my major**. Some of the classes for the core requirements are less interesting because they're not my personal preferences."

Q "**Most teachers treat you like a friend, and they are relaxed about general conversation**. The classes are very interesting; I feel like it is worth my time to do the homework. And even though I do a lot of work, most of the time I am interested enough to enjoy it."

Q "**The faculty is just like any other group of people**. There are some really good ones and some really bad ones. There's a really wide range, so everyone will iden- tify well with some and poorly with others. Even if you absolutely loathe them, though, you can understand why Colby hired them."

Q "I love most of my classes. My favorites use independent projects with topics completely up to the students. I've done things ranging from directing/acting in plays to neu- roimmunology. I particularly enjoyed realizing that I could choreograph molecule formation for Organic chemistry like a dance. **It's the freedom we're given that makes our classes interesting**."

Q "**The majority of teachers are extremely interested in their subject**, and it translates into their teaching. Most are also willing to help you in any way they can—during class, in office hours, or through email."

The College Prowler Take On...
Academics

Colby is a liberal arts school through and through. While we haven't eliminated core requirements entirely like some of the more progressive schoolss, we've whittled them down to seven "distribution requirements." All Colby students take an introductory English course as freshmen, and then have the rest of their time at school to take one class each in arts, historical studies, literature, quantitative reasoning, and social sciences. Colby also requires three semesters of a foreign language, two natural science classes, one of which must have a lab component, and two diversity credits, one focusing on the United States and another with a global perspective. These are completely easy to fulfill though. You can test out with AP scores, and if you still need to fulfill requirements you can take courses like "Math as a Liberal Art." Colby also features a unique 4-1-4 semester schedule. Students take four classes in the fall and the spring, and one class during January, called Jan-Plan.

The students are pretty much in agreement here: Colby's faculty is a pivotal part of academic life, and they make time here worthwhile. Caring and accessible, not to mention really, really smart, the professors are definitely one of Colby's biggest draws. Upperclassmen are always willing to rave about their favorite teachers, so talking to them is a great way to get a handle on which teachers are Colby legend, and which can be skipped, making it even easier to ensure a good academic experience. Academics, in general, are strong here. The English, government and biology departments are especially lauded.

The College Prowler™ Grade on
Academics: B+

A high Academics grade generally indicates that professors are knowledgeable, accessible, and genuinely interested in their students' welfare. Other determining factors include class size, how well professors communicate, and whether or not classes are engaging.

Local Atmosphere

The Lowdown On...
Local Atmosphere

Region:
Northeast

City, State:
Waterville, Maine

Setting:
Small town

Distance from Boston:
3-4 hours

Points of Interest:
Waterville Opera House
Railroad Square Cinema
(Waterville)
Maine State Museum
Old Fort Western (Augusta
Maine Maritime Museum (Bath)
Belgrade Lakes
Boothbay Railway Museum
(Boothbay Harbor)
Mt. Blue State Park
Bar Harbor
Acadia National Park
lighthouse (Pemaquid Point)
Museum of Fine Arts
Farnsworth Museum
Owls Head Transportation Museum
(Owls Head)

→

Closest Movie Theatres:

Railroad Square Cinema
17 Railroad Square, Waterville
Phone: (207) 873-6526

Hoyts Cinema Augusta 10
23 Marketplace Drive, Augusta
Phone: (207) 623-8183

Flagship Cinema
247 Kennedy Memorial Drive
Waterville
Phone: (207) 873 - 0033

Closest Shopping Malls:

Freeport outlets

Major Sports Teams:

Portland Sea Dogs
(Minor league baseball)

Portland Pirates (Hockey)

City Websites

www.watervillemainstreet.org
www.ci.waterville.me.us
www.watervillemaine.net

Did You Know?
5 Fun Facts about Waterville:
•Waterville is known as **Maine's Elm City.**

•Waterville is the home of the **Maine International Film Festival.**

•The upcoming movie Empire Falls, starring Helen Hunt, Ed Harris and Paul Newman, adapted from Richard Russo's Pulitzer Prize winning novel of the same name was filmed here at the beginning of the year. **Helen Hunt was occasionally spotted working out in the Colby athletic center.**

•Waterville has a **large French-Canadian population** and hosts great French-Canadian art festivals.

• The Colby campus was originally located in town, in between the river and the railroad tracks. It got too big and **moved up to Mayflower Hill** in the 1950s.

Local Atmosphere

> **"The Colby campus is generally viewed as separate from the surrounding area. Students have little interest in interacting with the local town and those of the town feel the same about Colby."**

Q "Not too many people spend that much time in Waterville. **If you go off campus it's usually to Portland, Freeport, Sugarloaf (the ski mountain) or to other mountains to hike or climb**. But Waterville provides everything we need; great pizza, pharmacies, hospitals, and a few awesome places to take the parents."

Q "It seems a little bleak at first, but you get used to it. **It contains everything you need in a college town**. Too much time can be spent meandering the aisles of Wal-Mart, for lack of other recreational outlets. If you become tired of flipping through the multiple Olsen Twin calendars, people watching can provide hours of solid entertainment. If nothing else, you may be able to spot the next suitable contestants for 'The Swan.'"

Q "The town we technically live in, and I say technically because campus is separated from the town, is a somewhat depressed Maine town, and our relationship with the people of Waterville is not at its best. Recently **some really great, funky restaurants have popped up**, though, as well as a coffee shop and café and a cool independent theatre. There is another college in town, but I don't know of any socializing that occurs between the two schools."

Q "So apparently **there's another school, Thomas College**, down the street. I've never met any students from there or even seen the campus. I've heard about it from some seniors, though."

Q "Waterville is a large town, but some may call it a small city, and it has a wide variety of fast food restaurants, and, of course, Wal-Mart, K-Mart, Shaw's and Hannaford. **The most visited spot is Wal-Mart**, other than that people tend to stay on campus."

Q "Waterville is small, quaint, and not what it was in the 1950s. What used to be an airport terminal is now a sleepy bus station. **Colby students don't get out much**."

Q "**The campus is rather isolated in our own 'Colby Bubble**.' It's nice to go downtown to get off campus for a while and get coffee at Jorgenson's. If you want to do any serious clothing shopping, though, you need to go to Augusta or Freeport."

Q "Colby is a small school, and the atmosphere is what you would expect. **It feels like a small community**. People know people, and care about what happens on campus. There are plenty of places to visit in the community if you like to volunteer, like the soup kitchen, animal shelter, and school. There are other schools nearby—Bowdoin and Bates, along with Thomas College."

Q "Don't be afraid of the townies! **Take a regular visit to Mainely Brew or the Bob In**. They only think you're stuck up if you actually are, so feel free to hang out at some of the dives and make a few friends."

Q "**The good things about Waterville are not obvious**. You have to hunt for them. You will find some great restaurants and a coffee shop, as well as a small movie theatre that shows a lot of independent films, and even an opera house."

   www.collegeprowler.com

Q "There aren't really any other schools in the immediate area, but Bates and Bowdoin are often visited for sports matches or concerts. Waterville is a pretty small town, but there are some good Thai restaurants and **the Wal-mart is the main attractions**."

Q "Waterville is relatively friendly. I have never had any bad or uncomfortable encounters. There is another college in Waterville, but Colby does not have much contact with Thomas College. **Waterville has exactly what you need—a Wal-mart, gas stations, and a few nice restaurants**."

Q "I was not initially thrilled with Waterville, but it has grown on me. **I think that the Waterville residents are a very nice group of people**. All the interaction I've had in the community has been positive for me."

Q **"Waterville itself has a very friendly, classic New England small town feel**. Thomas College is also in Waterville, but if it weren't for the signs in town giving direction I never would have known. Be careful in the South End of Waterville. It isn't terrible, but it is the worst section of town. Visit Acadia National Park and Bar Harbor. It's a bit of a drive to both of them, but they're both worth it."

Q **"Visit the Railroad Square Cinema**. It's a unique place for such a small town."

Local Atmosphere

Waterville is typically viewed as a tiny, quaint, and impoverished town. It's definitely a far cry from the Main St. college towns of many universities. While it provides Colby students with what they need, it is definitely not an attraction. Most students see a divide between the school and the town, although the Colby Volunteer Center, and groups like the South End Coalition are working hard to improve town-gown relations. Students also recognize some of the truly unique aspects of downtown Waterville. Railroad Square Cinema is a small, independent movie theatre well loved by students and faculty, and the Waterville Opera house is a cultural oasis in a town that sometimes seems to revolve around Wal-Mart.

No one comes to Colby College because they fall in love with Waterville. In fact, a lot of visiting students never even lay eyes on the town—Main St. is a five-minute drive away. There are rumors of their being of the other colleges in the area, but Colby students don't tend to interact with them.Waterville can be something of a culture shock, especially for students unaccustomed to Wal-Mart greeters and looking for trendy boutiques. Most students, though, accept its flaws, and find ways to enjoy getting off the hill every now and then.

The College Prowler™ Grade on

Local Atmosphere: C-

A high Local Atmosphere grade indicates that the area surrounding campus is safe and scenic. Other factors include nearby attractions, proximity to other schools, and the town's attitude toward students

Safety & Security

The Lowdown On...
Safety & Security

Number of Colby Police:
13

Colby Police Phone:
(207) 872-3345

Safety Services:
Jitney Service (transportation within Waterville), courtesy rides by security officers, Colby Check (property identification and marking), Lost and Found, safety whistles, party checks, emergency safety advisories

Health Services:
Basic medical services, on-site pharmaceuticals, breast exams, contraceptives (including emergency contraception), dietary consultation, pregnancy testing, STD and HIV testing, counseling services

Health Center Office Hours

Nurse coverage: 24 hours

Clinic hours: 24 hours

Did You Know?

Not a fun fact, but an important one: in September of 2003, a senior at Colby, Dawn Rossignol, was found dead about a mile from campus. **Her death was ruled a homicide** and her killer, Edward Hackett, a parolee from a prison in Utah, has been tried, found guilty, and sentenced to life in prison without parole.

Students Speak Out On...
Safety & Security

"There's good security on campus. I have always felt safe. Dawn's death I view as a very, very random tragic occurrence."

"In my three years at Colby **I have never felt unsafe or threatened by anything**. Colby does an excellent job of making students feel secure. My only complaint about security is that they are often too interested in breaking up parties and fining students."

"I've never felt in danger at Colby. **Security works incredibly hard to keep us safe**, and is always in the process of improving their equipment and methods. There's a student escort system, so no one has to walk anywhere by themselves. All you have to do is call the security office, and ask for the escort to walk you wherever you're going."

"**Security is very good at Colby**. They've recently improved it even more, and they're always around and available to help."

"Safety on campus is generally good, and I have always felt comfortable. Security does enjoy breaking up parties, but besides that **we have a secure atmosphere**."

"Security is pretty willing to help when you need it. **You can call for an escort at any time** and while they may not always be incredibly prompt, they'll always come and drive you where you need to go. Also, everyone is given whistles that they may use."

"**Security is excellent**. I feel very safe."

Q "**I've always felt safe on campus**. Once, when I couldn't find my car in the parking lot, the security officer on patrol pulled up in his SUV, and helped me because he didn't want me lingering in the lot."

Q "Security is nice, but **they think they are all undercover FBI agents**."

Q "**Security is completely adequate** and a bit bothersome on the weekends, but there hasn't been a time when I've felt unsafe on campus."

Q "The security is always present. **Security officers are constantly patrolling in their cars**; I see someone from the staff several times a day. I can honestly say there were only one or two times throughout the school year that I didn't feel safe."

Q "**I feel safe going anywhere** I want on campus."

The College Prowler Take On...
Safety & Security

It's a testament to how much Colby students trust security that absolutely everyone seems to feel completely safe on campus, even after the tragic (and well-remembered) death of Dawn Rossignol in the fall of 2003. Colby's isolated location is certainly a reason for this sense of safety. Also, Colby security is very visible and very well known. Most students can tell you the names and nicknames of at least one security officer, and it's not uncommon for students to stop and chat with whichever officer is prowling around outside dances. Also, students trust each other. Most feel comfortable leaving their books and bags in the library while they meet friends at a dining hall for dinner, and there are very few reports of stolen items. If you lose something, chances are you'll either find it right where you left it or get a phone call from the person who found it.

Despite the tragic events of the fall that perhaps should have instilled more fear into the student body, Colby is viewed as a very safe campus. Security's constant presence was especially reassuring in the weeks after Dawn's death. Students tend to be on good terms with security (unless they're breaking up parties, which does happen, see the campus strictness section), and on good terms with each other, which makes everyone feel safe on campus.

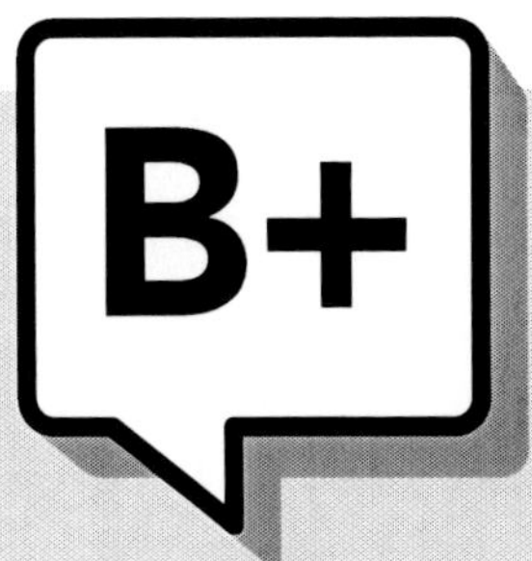

The College Prowler™ Grade on

Safety & Security: B+

A high grade in Safety & Security means that students generally feel safe, campus police are visible, blue-light phones and escort services are readily available, and safety precautions are not overly necessary.

Computers

The Lowdown On...
Computers

High-Speed Network?
Yes.

Wireless Network?
In the library only

Numbers of Computers:
77

Operating Systems:
PC and MAC

24-Hour Labs
Miller Street, Lovejoy Lab

Free Software:
Nothing's free, but Microsoft Word is covered by tuition. Also, Colby has purchased several software packages for download, including Oracle Calendar, EndNote 7, SOPHOS, Fetch 4.03 (for Mac OSX only), Better Telnet (for Mac only) and TeraTerm (for Windows only)

Charge to Print?
No

Computers

> **"Although I have always had a laptop in my room, I've found that I do most of my work in Colby's computer labs. They're rarely crowded, and it's often easier to concentrate than a noisy dorm."**

Q "Basically everyone brings their own computers, but we still use the computer labs—**the network is great**."

Q **"I would definitely bring my own computer**. There are some great labs, but they are not open twenty-four hours, and they are often crowded."

Q "The computer labs are usually crowded at crunch times, like midterms and finals, but besides that you can always find a spot. **Most people do have their own computers**, and since everyone is given Ethernet in their room it is definitely nice to have your own. If you don't own one I don't think it would be a huge problem."

Q "I work in the Miller Library, and the computer lab there is only crowded during exam week. Most of the time it's pretty empty. **Bring your own computer** anyway since it makes life more convenient."

Q "The computer network is well kept and provides lots of services. Almost all of the bandwidth is devoted to web surfing capabilities, so pages are very rarely slow in loading. **We are provided with access to all kinds of scholarly journal websites**, making research a lot easier."

Q "**I'd recommend having your own computer**. The library labs are usually only full around finals, but the student network does allow for easy transfer of viruses. Our student computer services, though, are incredibly helpful about ridding your computer of viruses when need be."

Q "The computer network is great. **There are several computers on campus,** from the computer labs in the libraries to the computers in the club offices. I would say only bring your computer for the convenience of having a computer on hand. If it's not that important, don't bring it. The labs can become crowded at certain times, but if you build a schedule, and do your work around those busy times you should be fine."

Q "The only time that the computer labs are crowded is during the reading period before finals. Even then you can find a computer to use if you look for five minutes. **Even with the labs readily accessible your own computer is a really good idea**. Some of the dorms are a bit of a walk from the labs, so the convenience is nice in the dead of winter. Also, you can't just leave a project sitting on a lab computer, and take a break because all lab computer memories are wiped upon restarting."

Q "Computers at Colby are plentiful, and almost always free and working. **I've been without my computer for a few weeks, and it wasn't too bad.** It's nice to have your own computer if you need a lot of quiet when you work (although if you have a loud roommate it won't matter anyway)."

Q "The computer labs can be crowded during the day if classes are using them. Since there aren't computers in the residence halls, **it's a lot more convenient to bring your own.**"

Q "**The computers are good enough to burn CDs,** and that's all that matters."

Q **"The network is abysmal**. Any virus you see making waves on the news, Colby has. And they will all kill your network connection intermittently until ITS finally gets around to fixing the computers of those that are too stupid to fix them themselves."

Q "I enjoy having my own computer, but there are plenty of public computers available all over campus. **You can pretty much always find a computer when you need it**."

The College Prowler Take On...
Computers

There are plenty of computers sprinkled throughout campus for general use, although the labs can get quite crowded around finals. Many students bring computers, but it's up to you to decide if you want a laptop or a desktop, a PC or a Mac. Colby only has wireless Internet in Miller Library, so you do have to plug in when you're in your dorm. Usually this works pretty well, and it's great to be able to send files quickly over the network. It's not foolproof though, and the network has an ugly tendency to fail during the most critical times (like finals).

Having your own computer is definitely a nice convenience, especially because nobody wants to be walking from their room to a computer lab at 2 a.m. in a blinding snowstorm. It is also more convenient for those who are just plain lazy, and don't feel like going to the lab. But if you can't bring a computer on your own, you probably won't suffer too grievously. Colby students do seem especially prone to viruses, and technological help seems to be pretty hit or miss. Most students recommend bringing your own laptop, and getting great anti-virus protection (or bring a Mac – they're less likely to get viruses).

The College Prowler™ Grade on

Computers: B-

A high grade in Computers designates that computer labs are available, the computer network is easily accessible, and the campus' computing technology is up-to-date.

Facilities

The Lowdown On...
Facilities

Student Center:
Cotter Union

Athletic Center:
Alfond Athletic Center

Libraries:
3 - Art & Music, Science, General

Popular Places to Chill:
The Spa
The Pub
The Pugh Center
The Street

Campus Size:
714 acres

What Is There to Do On Campus?

A huge on-campus art museum, athletic center, coffeehouse, bar, and snack shop make it easy to find something to do (and spend money) right on campus. Movies are shown in lecture halls or the coffeehouse on weekends, and there are often student performances in Runnals Union (the theatre and dance building), Lorimer Chapel, or Page Commons (in the Student Union).

Movie Theatre on Campus?

No, but some lecture rooms are used to show films on a pretty regular basis.

Bar on Campus?

The Blue Light Pub in Cotter Union.

Coffeehouse on Campus?

Coffee Cart in the Miller Library.

Favorite Things to Do:

While Colby students are usually content to talk to each other wherever they happen to meet in between classes, Colby's facilities are put to good use as well. The gym's popular, especially in the late afternoon and early evening. When the weather is nice, students flock outdoors to Johnson Pond or one of the many grassy, sunny spots. In the evenings, the on-campus Pub is typically packed (even during the week).

Facilities

> **"Colby is uber-pristine—they take great care of all the facilities and buildings, and are always trying to offer the best to the students. If anything falls below par, they re-do it."**

Q "I have always been pleased with Colby's facilities. **The college is constantly upgrading and improving**."

Q "**Some buildings are old and crappy** but others are new and state-of-the-art. There's a wide variety. Overall, the buildings are up-to-date on technology, and they are going through a lot of renovations."

Q "The facilities are beautiful. Colby is very good about renovating and consequently everything looks fairly new and well kept. **The athletic center is beautiful**, and tons of people use it, from varsity athletes to others who just want to get in shape."

Q "**The facilities are awesome**, and the athletic center is great. I use the gym all the time, and honestly it is the nicest one I've been to. The pool is wonderful, as are the basketball court, hockey rink, track, and aerobics room. There's a writer's center for people who want help with term papers or anything written. I've used it, and it's great. The health center is wonderful too. The nurses there can help you with anything."

Q "The student center looks plastic and fake. **The Math and Physics building looks like a prison**, but the rest of the campus is beautiful."

Q "**The library has too many steps**. It's like a Himalayan trek getting to the third floor of Miller, and by then one is too tired to study and instead slumps into those comfy chairs, and has a three hour nap, or so I've heard."

Q "The student center is not a popular place to hang out. It's a nice building, but for some reason people don't really seem to use it besides getting their mail. **The academic buildings, libraries, laboratories, and gym are all very nice**."

Q "**The athletic center is amazing and huge**. There is a pool, ice hockey rink, a basketball court, a weight room with awesome equipment, an indoor track, and an exercise/yoga room. As for the student center—I love it. I hang out there a lot whenever I don't want to be confined to my room or someone else's."

Q "**All the facilities are top notch**. When it comes to physical buildings and their contents, I couldn't ask for more. There are really only a few problems I have with them. One big one is that the athletic center is as far away from the dorms as it can be. And as for the student center, it's only a student center in name. The only reason students go there at all is because it houses the post office and the ATM."

Q "**The facilities on campus are state-of-the-art**. I remember when I first visited Colby it looked like someone daily polished the lettering on every building. The athletic center is very nice; it gets crowded at high times (four or five in the afternoon) when everyone goes to work out, but if you go at the off times you'll be fine. I love the town hall theme in Page Commons, where many speakers and dances are held."

The College Prowler Take On...
Facilities

Some students claim to have chosen to come to Colby because all the buildings matched. The buildings and landscaping are definitely top-quality, and the view from the Miller Library steps is nothing short of breathtaking. The athletic center is well liked and well used—sometimes a little too well used. It's quite a challenge to find an exercise machine after classes get out in the late afternoon. And, although Miller Library is very picturesque and (sometimes controversially) well lit, many students choose not to study there in favor of the brighter, more welcoming Olin Science Library. Cotter Union is a huge building and includes Page Commons (for dances, lectures, and other big events), the Pugh Center, the Spa, the Pub, the on-campus post-office, mailboxes and an ATM.

Despite Cotter Union's potential as a gathering place, though, most of Colby's action takes place in dorm rooms or in the dining halls. Although Cotter Union is a great place to sell tickets to events, or to try to get people to sign petitions, it is not a place where people stop and chat for long. The Pugh Center has a similar problem. It's well furnished and comfortable, but no one hangs out there. The campus is small enough to render a central meeting spot practically unnecessary. The beauty of the buildings is a great way to attract people to the school, but kids prefer to get together elsewhere.

The College Prowler™ Grade on
Facilities: B

A high Facilities grade indicates that the campus is aesthetically pleasing and well-maintained; facilities are state-of-the-art, and libraries are exceptional. Other determining factors include the quality of both athletic and student centers and an abundance of things to do on campus.

Campus Dining

The Lowdown On...
Campus Dining

Freshman Meal Plan Requirement?

Yes

Meal Plan Average Cost:

Included in tuition

Places to Grab a Bite with Your Meal Plan

Dana Dining Hall:

Generic dining hall with pizza, burgers, sandwiches, salad, and the longest hours

Foss Dining Hall

The "gourmet" dining hall known for its vegetarian and vegan fare

Robert's Dining Hall:

Affectionately referred to as Bob's, this dining hall offers more greasy-spoon fare

Student Favorites

The Spa, the Pub

Campus Dining

> **"The food is amazing—I never get sick of it. Foss has, hands down, the best atmosphere, and really the most quality food (including the best salad bar). Dana and Bob's are fairly tasty, too, but not quite as exciting. The omelet and grilled cheese bars are amazingly one-of-a kind."**

Q "For college food, Colby does pretty well. I have always been pleased, and surprisingly **impressed by the selection and quality**."

Q "The food, in my opinion, is very good. **I love that there are three dining halls** because you get a wide variety of food to choose from at any given meal."

Q "**All of the dining halls are good**. Where you eat says a lot about you. I like that they all have good salad bars, and there is always fresh fruit. The desserts are dangerous, though. Beware: there are so many, and they all taste so good!"

Q "**The food on campus is extraordinarily good**. All three dining halls serve different, but high quality, food. Just be careful to know exactly what you're eating at Foss or you might get a nasty surprise. After a year or so the food can get a little monotonous, but there's huge potential for mixing the foods to keep things interesting. My favorite is cutting up the Sunday night chicken fingers into a salad, and pairing it with a mug full of root beer and a scoop of ice cream. Creativity is the difference between dorm food and cuisine."

Q "The food, honestly, is really good. And yes, I am talking about the dining halls. **It's all-you-can-eat, three meals a day, seven days a week**. I think it makes a huge difference that we have such good food—life is more enjoyable."

Q "There is always generic fast food at Dana, but **I would recommend Foss to the adventuresome eater**. The food on campus is quite good, although the menu can be quite repetitive: Sunday nights are always chicken fingers."

Q "Foss is for the crunchies, **Bob's is for the sports teams, and Dana is for everyone else.** But, with that said, Bob's has great wraps at lunch, and Dana has the longest hours, so nothing is in concrete."

Q "Colby's food is amazing. **You will gain weight if you come here.**"

Q "Eventually I grew tired of the food, but I can't complain. **I am grateful for the variety**. Also, the dining halls are spacious, but can get crowded sometimes. The dining halls are very well kept by an amazing team of dedicated and diligent dining hall staff members."

Q "The food on campus is great; there are no complaints here. Of the three dining halls on campus, I only eat at Foss. **There is great food—it's fresh, and always has vegetarian options.**"

Q **"Bob's is depressing—it's like eating in an unlit cave.** Dana is evil because of its tempting, eye-snatching pizza and fast food."

Q "Food on campus is awesome. **You do get sick of eating it all the time**, even though it is good."

Q "I can't stress enough how amazing the food here is. **I can't think of a restaurant that does a better job than the Colby dining halls**. They have a nice selection, and there is something for everyone—vegetarian, vegan and carnivorous. All the food is high quality and fresh—there is no canned stuff, and every meal is a joy here."

Q "**The food is awesome**! I have visited a lot of other colleges and nothing compares."

Dining is integral to Colby social life, and the individual characteristics of the three dining halls are part of what defines campus politics. Tables in the dining halls are big, as they are meant for large groups of friends, and they usually end up overcrowded anyway. Lots of social interaction happens over dining-hall food, and it's not too much of a stretch to say that friendships have formed and ended due to dining hall preference. Foss-lovers praise the gourmet and vegan fare, but can be blind to the small size and crowdedness of their favorite dining hall. Bob's fans are devoted to the pasta and grilled cheese bars, but can overlook the dismal atmosphere and wimpy salad bar. Dana is surprisingly middle-of-the-road, although students who live in Dana love the convenience (and consequently never leave their building).

Three dining halls does feel like there are too few by the end of the school year, especially during the long month of January when Foss is (tragically) closed. But food is an important part of the Colby experience. The food is good, the desserts are phenomenal, and the dining halls provide a great social outlet, especially since meal plans are required.

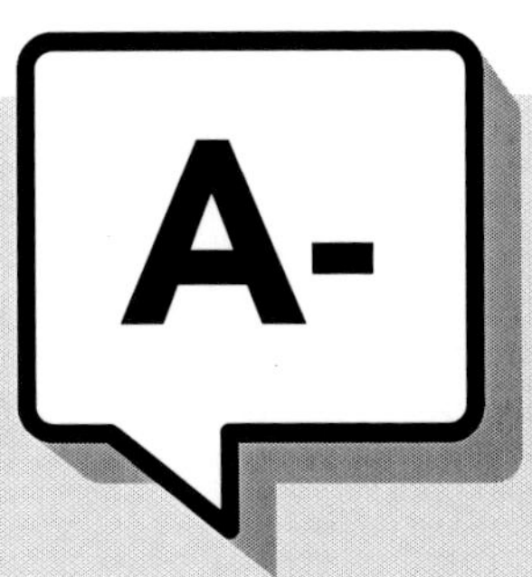

The College Prowler™ Grade on

Campus Dining: A-

Our grade on Campus Dining addresses the quality of both school-owned dining halls and independent on-campus restaurants as well as the price, availability, and variety of food.

Off-Campus Dining

The Lowdown On...
Off-Campus Dining

Restaurant Prowler: Popular Places to Eat!

Applebee's
Food: American
Address: 251 Kennedy Memorial Drive, Waterville
Phone: (207) 872-6702
Price: $11-$20 per person

Asian Café
Food: Asian
Address: 69 Bay St., Waterville
Phone: (207) 877-6688
Cool Features: Delivery Available
Price: $11-$20 per person

Big G's
Food: Pizza, Subs & Sandwiches
Address: Benton Ave., Winslow
Phone: (207) 873-7808
Price: $11-$20 per person

Bread Box Café
Food: American
Address: 137 Main St., Waterville
Phone: (207) 873-4090
Price: $15-$30 per person

Burger King
Food: Fast Food
Address: 144 College Ave., Waterville; 465 Kennedy

Burger King (*Continued...*)

Memorial Drive, Waterville

Phone: (207) 872-6848; (207) 877-07772

Price: $10 and under per person

Freedom Café

Food: Southern/Soul

Address: 18 Silver St., Waterville

Phone: (207) 8759-8742

Price: $21-$30 per person

Friendly's

Food: American

Address: 373 Main St., Waterville

Phone: (207) 872-4598

Price: $11-$20 per person

Gifford's Ice Cream

Food: Desert

Address: 170 Silver St., Waterville

Phone: (207) 872-6631

Cool Features: The outdoor ice-cream shop also has mini-golfing and batting cages

Price: $10 and under per person

Grand Central Café

Food: Pizza, Subs & Sandwiches

Address: 10 Railroad Square, Waterville

Phone: (207) 872-9135

Price: $10 and under per person

Last Unicorn

Food: American

Address: 8 Silver St. Waterville

Phone: (207) 873 - 6378

Price: $25 - $25 per person

McDonald's

Food: Fast Food

Address: 435 Kennedy Memorial Drive, Waterville; 336 Upper Main St., Waterville; 3 China Rd.

Phone: (207) 873-6366 ; (207) 872-8212 ; (207) 873-6400

Price: $10 and under per person

Pad Thai

Food: Oriental

Address: 98 College Ave., Waterville

Phone: (207) 861-8895

Price: $11-$20 per person

Sllver St. Tavern

Food: American

Address: 2 Sllver St., Waterville

Phone: (207) 873 - 8323

Price: $11 - $20 per person

Waterville House of Pizza

Address: 139 Main St., Waterville

Phone: (207) 873-4300

Best Pizza:
Big G's, Waterville

Best Chinese:
Pad Thai, Asian Café

Best Breakfast:
Bread Box Café, The Last Unicorn, The Freedom Café

Closest Grocery Store
Hannaford Food and Drug
19 Elm Plazas
Waterville
Phone: (207) 877-0700

Shaw's Supermarket
251 Kennedy Memorial Drive
Waterville
Phone: (207) 873-6224

Did You Know?

Late-Night Snacking

For late night munchies, hit up a Waterville House of Pizza or Spanky's Pizza

Student Favorites
Bread Box Café

Big G's

Gifford's Ice Cream

Pad Thai

Freedom Café

Grand Central Café

Waterville House of Pizza

Students Speak Out On...
Off-Campus Dining

"Although campus food is not too shabby, everyone needs a break. My favorite off-campus spots are the famed Pad Thai (a student favorite), and the Bread Box (for when you're being treated)."

Q "**Grand Central Café is by far the best place to go for pizza**, or dinner for that matter. The service is slow, but the brick of bread is delicious."

Q "Pad Thai is absolutely delicious (and they love Colby kids), The Last Unicorn is very quality (great place for parents), **Silver Street has the best meat**, and the Bread Box is also very tasty."

Q "There are a couple great Thai places, a few seafood places, a good soul-food place, and a couple nice, traditional American restaurants. **Colby students have a peculiar and rather unanimous affection for Pad Thai.**"

Q "There are a few really good restaurants in town: Pad Thai, which is the most popular place for Thai food; **the Freedom Café has excellent food that tends to be southern and home-made**; the Breadbox Café, a really nice little place with a great atmosphere and amazing food; Jorgenson's, an adorable little café with sandwiches, and a huge variety of coffee, and Big G's, which has excellent and ENORMOUS sandwiches and breakfasts.

Q "No Colby experience is complete without **visiting Pad Thai** and Asian Café."

Q "**The Freedom Café is a must**; I just love the Southern cooking."

Q "I recommend getting your Asian food fix from Pad Thai instead of Asian Café. Not only is Pad Thai much better, but the prices are usually lower. **Asian Café is easier if you don't have a car because they deliver.** I recommend Waterville House of Pancakes and Big G's for large, inexpensive breakfasts."

Q "For a small town, Waterville has this covered! **We've got Big G's for HUGE and creative sandwiches** (try the Zonker Harriss), Asian Café and Pad Thai for all things Asian, and Freedom Café for huge portions of truly excellent southern cooking."

Q "Pad Thai is good, **Waterville House of Pizza is a good place to order from at 1 a.m.**, and the Last Unicorn and the Freedom Café are good places to go when your parents are paying."

Q "**There are a ton of great restaurants**. You just have to know how to get to them since they're not right next to the highway."

Off-Campus Dining

You'll be hard-pressed to find a Colby student who doesn't have an inexplicable and undying love for Pad Thai. The small, often crowded, hole-in-the-wall Thai restaurant is easily the most popular in Waterville, which is quite the accomplishment in a city full of great restaurants. The food is definitely Waterville's biggest attraction (we sure don't have shopping). Although restaurants are often far from campus or difficult to find (Big G's is particularly elusive), students are always willing to venture into the Waterville wilds and find great food. Not all the restaurants are great. Applebee's, Ruby Tuesday, and Friendly's are far from unique, and many of the better restaurants are far too pricey for a modest college-student budget. Getting people to deliver food is tricky, too. Most of the pizza places will make doorway appearances, but you might have to wait an hour or two on busy weekend nights. Asian Café delivers as well, but it's kind of pricey.

Although on-campus dining halls are great, they get old, and Waterville rises to the needs of bored Colby students. There are pricier restaurants with amazing food to enjoy with your parent and less-expensive restaurants with equally amazing food to enjoy with your friends. Waterville House of Pizza will deliver gourmet pizzas with innovative toppings to your dorm and Mullen's will bring you three pizzas for dirt-cheap. The popular spots get crowded and continual eating out will burn holes in your wallet, but in a city that often has little to offer Colby students, the off-campus dining scene is pretty phenomenal.

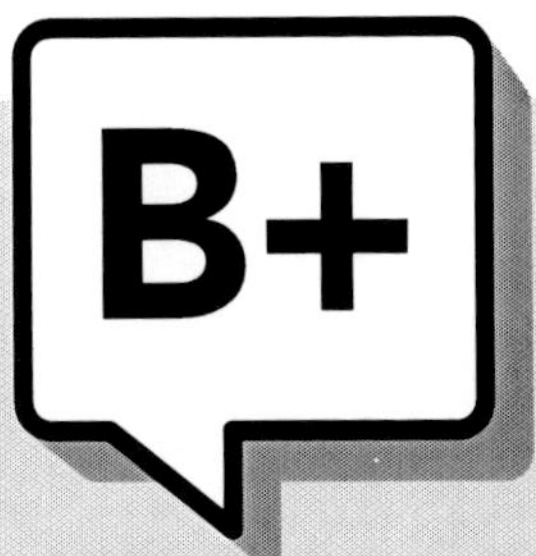

The College Prowler™ Grade on

Off-Campus Dining: B+

A high off-campus dining grade implies that off-campus restaurants are affordable, accessible, and worth visiting. Other factors include the variety of cuisine and the availability of alternative options (vegetarian, vegan, Kosher, etc.).

Campus Housing

The Lowdown On...
Campus Housing

Room Types:

Residence Halls have a variety of rooms. Singles, doubles, two-room doubles, one or two-room triples, quads, five-person suites and six-person suites are all available. Quads, five-person and six-person suites have their own bathrooms, as do a few doubles and triples. For the most part, though, students living in singles, doubles and triples share a central bathroom located near their rooms. Seniors may elect to live in on-campus apartments, which include a variety of really luxurious suites (including a two-story six-person suite).

Best Dorms:

- AMS
- Averill
- Johnson and Mary Low

Worst Dorms:

- Heights
- Frat Row
- Hillside

Dormitory Residences

All dorms contain approximately fifty-five percent female students and forty-five percent males students. Approximately thirty percent of any dorm is first-year students and sophomores, twenty-one percent juniors, and nineteen percent seniors.

Anthony (the 'A' part of AMS)

Floors: 3

Total Occupancy: 54

Bathrooms: 6

Co-Ed: Yes

Room Types: singles, one-room doubles, six-person suites

Special Features: two lounges, laundry facilities

Averill

Floors: 4

Total Occupancy: 61

Bathrooms: 8

Co-Ed: Yes

Room Types: singles, one-room doubles, one-, two- and three-room triples, quads

Special Features: lounge with study rooms and a kitchen, laundry facilities

Coburn

Floors: 4

Total Occupancy: 87

Bathrooms: 8

Co-Ed: Yes

Room Types: singles, one-room doubles, one-room triples

Coburn (*Continued...*)

Special Features: quiet dorm that has extended quiet hours, lounge with fireplace, laundry facilities

Dana

Floors: 3

Total Occupancy: 168

Bathrooms: 12

Co-Ed: Yes

Room Types: singles, one-room doubles, five-person suites

Special Features: in the same building as the Dana dining hall. Has a lounge and laundry facilities

Drummond (one of the frat row dorms)

Floors: 4

Total Occupancy: 43

Bathrooms: 4

Co-Ed: Yes

Room Types: singles, one-room doubles, one-room triples

Special Features: lounge with fireplace, laundry facilities

East Quad

Floors: 4

Total Occupancy: 120

Bathrooms: 8

Co-Ed: Yes

Room Types: singles, one- and two-room doubles, two-room triples

Special Features: chem.-free. Has a lounge and laundry facilities

Foss

Floors: 3

Total Occupancy: 86

Bathrooms: 4

Co-Ed: Yes

Room Types: singles, one-room doubles, two-room triples, quads, 6-person suites

Special Features: in the same building as the Foss dining hall—has laundry facilities

Heights

Floors: 3

Total Occupancy: 100

Bathrooms: 6

Co-Ed: Yes

Room Types: singles, one- and two-room doubles, quads

Special Features: has a huge lounge used for popular and well-attended dances, as well as smaller lounges on each floor and laundry facilities.

Leonard (one of the Hillside dorms)

Floors: 3

Total Occupancy: 47

Bathrooms: 2

Co-Ed: Yes

Room Types: one-room doubles, one- and two-room triples

Special Features: lounge, laundry facilities

Marriner (one of the Hillside dorms)

Floors: 2

Total Occupancy: 44

Bathrooms: 2

Co-Ed: Yes

Room Types: one-room doubles, one-room triples

Special Features: lounge, laundry facilities

Mary Low

Floors: 3

Total Occupancy: 81

Bathrooms: 6

Co-Ed: Yes

Room Types: singles, one- and two-room doubles, one- and two-room triples, quads

Special Features: chem.-free (no alcohol or drugs). Houses the campus coffeehouse, the Annex (a six-person suite on the first floor) and the Co-op (a collection of rooms on the first floor which share a kitchen). Has a lounge with a piano and laundry facilities

Mitchell (the 'M' part of AMS)

Floors: 3

Total Occupancy: 50

Bathrooms: 6

Co-Ed: Yes

Room Types: singles, one-room doubles, quads

Special Features: two lounges, laundry facilities

Schupf (the 'S' part of AMS)

Floors: 3

Total Occupancy: 45

Bathrooms: 4

Co-Ed: Yes

Room Types: singles, one-room doubles, five-person, six-person suites

Special Features: three lounges, laundry facilities

Treworgy (one of the frat row dorms)

Floors: 3

Total Occupancy: 38

Bathrooms: 2

Co-Ed: Yes

Room Types: one-room doubles, six-person suite

Special Features: lounge with fireplace, laundry facilities

West Quad

Floors: 3

Total Occupancy: 106

Bathrooms: 6

Co-Ed: Yes

Room Types: singles, one- and two-room doubles, two-room triples

Special Features: lounge, laundry facilities

Williams (one of the Hillside dorms)

Floors: 3

Total Occupancy: 48

Bathrooms: 2

Co-Ed: Yes

Room Types: one-room doubles, one-room triples, quads

Special Features: lounge, laundry facilities, chem.-free, occasionally referred to as "Wild Bill's"

Woodman

Floors: 4

Total Occupancy: 94

Bathrooms: 8

Co-Ed: Yes

Room Types: singles, one- and two-room doubles, two-room triples

Special Features: in the same building as the Foss dining hall. Has a lounge with a TV and a kitchen and laundry facilities

Undergrads on Campus:

94%

University-Owned Apartments

One building

Bed Type

Extra-long twins, can be lofted if you ask nicely

Available for Rent

Micro-fridges

Cleaning Service?

In the public bathrooms

What You Get

Dormitories

Bed, dresser, closet, desk, chair, as many Ethernet connections as there are people in the room, telephone jack, cable TV jack

Percentage of Students in Singles:

35%

Percentage of Students in Doubles:

43%

Percentage of Students in Triples/Suites:

13%

Percentage of Students in Apartments:

N/A

Students Speak Out On...
Campus Housing

"Since the re-modeling and re-vamping of the dorms on campus there really aren't any dorms that are truly awful. Heights is ugly, but has two room doubles, and is close to a dining hall. The Hillside dorms (or 'ugly white buildings') aren't so hot, but the rooms are big. Frat Row has smaller rooms, but isn't bad for location"

Q "The dorms are adequate. **Some of the dorms have been newly renovated**, and they are nicer than others. Johnson, Averill and AMS are really nice; Treworgy and Grossman I would avoid."

Q "**The dorms totally vary**. There are old frat houses and new buildings that feel like hotels—each has its ups and downs. The frat row dorms are kind of on the shabby side, but are more social. The new dorms have nice bathrooms, but can be less social."

Q "**The dorms are spacious and comfortable**, but there are some that are tiny. Dorms on frat row don't have the best bathrooms. All are equipped with one or more common rooms, kitchens, televisions, and vending machines. The laundry rooms are not bad, but can be a hassle if there is only one for the twenty-eight people in a dorm."

Q "**Dorms are generally decent**. At such a small school I find that you spend little time in your dorm room because it's so easy to visit friends and travel around campus."

Q "The buildings are pristine, and the dorms can be in really nice condition too, although some of the rooms can be miniscule. It would be nice if there was more suite-type living. **Heights is pretty far away, but there are always parties there**. Frat row is in the worst condition, but the dorms are so small that everyone becomes friends. There are ups and downs to all of the dorms."

Q "**Sophomore year I had an amazing suite with my own private study** and a common room intimate enough to host fondue parties, but big enough to dance in."

Q "The dorms are really great. **Almost no one lives off campus**. Foss, Mary Low, Coburn, AMS, Averill and Johnson are the nicest buildings. West Quad, East Quad and Johnson have the best location. The frat row dorms are indisputably the worst buildings; Heights isn't far behind. Frat row, Hillside, and Foss all have bad locations. The Senior Apartments are the best in every category, but they're only open to seniors."

Q "The dorms do vary, but overall they tend to be very nice. Of course, the newest (or newly renovated) dorms, like AMS, Foss, Woodman, Averill, and Johnson, are all beautiful inside. The college is in the process of renovating the small dorms on Frat Row, which tend to have smaller rooms and older facilities. **The Hillside dorms are not quite as nice,** but they are very social and a lot of fun to live in."

Q "Chem.-free dorms are nice because you don't have to deal with people puking in the bathrooms. **Avoid Williams. It has a nice sense of community, but is not too exciting**."

Q "Some dorms are pretty nice and some look horrible. The nice ones are the chem.-free and quiet dorms—**the worst are on frat row**."

Q "The dorms are what you make of them. I lived in Williams, which was not the best place to be. There are some very nice dorms, though. Even though I was in a gross dorm, I had a great HR and there were never any problems. Some dorms have more issues than others (avoid Dana and Foss because of the fire alarms), and some are newer than others. If you like quiet or chem.-free, we have that too. **All the dorms are pretty close to all the academic buildings**. It is worth living on campus."

Q "**I love the dorms**. I lived in Hillside and I'm going to do so again next year. It's not the appearance that makes the dorm, it's the people."

Q "**I really like the chem.-free option**—they are clean and friendly."

Campus Housing

Dorms are pretty hit-or-miss. There aren't really any phenomenal rooms, but nothing's too abysmal either. Dorms are renovated on a twenty-year rotating schedule, so no building is more than twenty years old, and something is always being updated. People in Mary Low might say they'd never give up their nice bathrooms and live on frat row, while the frat row residents would never move to a big dorm, and give up the sense of community and fun the row has to offer. Chem.-free is a surprisingly popular living option, and carries no stigma whatsoever. Many claim that one of the best things about Colby's housing system is that everyone lives together. All buildings are co-ed by room, rather than by floor, and there is no themed housing or freshmen housing. Freshmen live with seniors, live with guys, live with girls, live with international students and live with Mainers.

The dorms are not five-star hotel quality, but there are no buildings that stand out as really great or really awful. Ever-optimistic Colby students can find something great to say about any dorm on campus, while acknowledging the inconveniences. Most students focus on the social nature of the buildings, rather than the actual facilities. Colby provides students with the bare basics, and they are adequate. The people living in the dorms are often what make them special and unique.

C+

The College Prowler™ Grade on

Campus Housing: C+

A high Campus Housing grade indicates that dorms are clean, well-maintained, and spacious. Other determining factors include variety of dorms, proximity to classes, and social atmosphere.

Off-Campus Housing

The Lowdown On...
Off-Campus Housing

Undergrads in Off-Campus Housing:

6%

Average Rent for a House:

$250-$350/month. ten and twelve month leases.

Popular Areas:

On the lakes

Best Time to Look for a Place

Fall of junior year (if you want to live off campus as a senior)

Off-Campus Housing

"Students usually stick to on-campus housing until senior year. This is one of my favorite aspects of Colby—everyone is always around and on campus. By senior year you can choose to live off campus and experience something new."

Q **"Housing off campus is convenient,** but I don't think it's worth it."

Q "Most students live on campus. The people **I know who live off campus either really love it or really hate it.** They all appreciate the freedom from college rules, but at the same time rant about the rent."

Q **"I understand it to be very difficult,** mostly because you have to have a car, and find roommates who want to live off campus. Roommates are hard to find, because it's a lot more fun to live on campus. For one thing, you can always go back to your room between classes. The best part about living on campus is being immersed in everything. Your best friends are just down the hall and you can find something to do at the drop of a hat."

Q "Some of the off-campus housing is convenient, but a lot of the houses are more than a ten-minute drive from campus. **I would rather live on campus.**"

Q "Most people live on campus, and **if you want to live off campus you have to apply to do so**. Usually seniors and juniors are the people who live off campus, and it's really crucial that you have a car because there are not too many houses immediately surrounding the college. I prefer living at school—you can always go to the parties off-campus, and it seems more practical to live a five-minute walk away from classes."

Q "**Get heat and all utilities if possible**. My roomies and I ended up paying $300 or more a month for heating oil—ouch."

The College Prowler Take On...
Off-Campus Housing

Most people (especially underclassmen) see off-campus living as a party scene, and that's about it. Colby students tend to live on-campus. Off-campus housing is unique. There aren't apartments, but houses rented year-after-year by Colby students. Off-campus housing is included in the housing lottery at the end of the year, and it's rare that sophomores qualify to live off campus. Typically, only a few seniors actually rent houses (although there's been an increasing trend in past years). Students who feel trapped on campus, or who want a break from the rules and security, will move into houses their senior year. They can remain on a meal plan, receiving 100 meals per semester. Other than that, the school offers little support or guidance. Students who qualify for off-campus housing get a list of contacts, but are pretty much on their own beyond that. Houses can be old or new and close to campus or far.

Off-campus housing is an enigmatic part of Colby College life. Everyone, even freshmen, head to off-campus houses like "the Lodge," or "Paradise," for parties. Only the seniors who live off-campus really know what it's like though. The school does not really publicize this alternate living option, and those who want to escape campus life typically prefer on-campus alternatives like the senior apartments or the co-op.

The College Prowler™ Grade on

Off-Campus Housing: D

A high grade in Off-Campus Housing indicates that apartments are of high quality, close to campus, affordable, and easy to secure.

Diversity

The Lowdown On...
Diversity

American Indian:
0.3%

Asian or Pacific Islander:
4.7%

African American:
1.9%

Hispanic:
2.9%

White:
83.4%

International:
6.8%

Out of State:
87.9%

Political Activity

Although many students would identify themselves as left leaning, the conservatives on campus are very vocal and well organized. There are a handful of very vocal, very liberal activist-types who go to protests and organize campus events. Racial awareness week and social class awareness week were particularly notable, as well as an extremely well organized diversity conference. Many students, though, are inactive politically.

Gay Tolerance

One student wrote: "Some gay kids never have a problem at Colby, because they only need to hold their partner's hand to feel content while they wear their popped-up collars and claim to be just like normal people." In general, the campus is very supportive of gay-rights issues, but tends to get uncomfortable if things get too loud

Economic Status

Most Colby students seem to come from very well-off backgrounds. Although the school is economically diverse, these differences aren't easy to see, which contributes to the (perhaps erroneous) perception of the school as entirely populated by rich, white, New Englanders.

Minority Clubs

The Pugh Center, located within the student center building, houses many diversity-oriented clubs. Students Organized Against Racism (SOAR), Students Organized for Black and Hispanic Unity (SOBHU), The Bridge (gay-straight alliance), and all the religious groups are a few of the twenty or so clubs that have offices, and safe spaces in the Pugh Center. The Pugh Community Board works to facilitate dialogue between these groups, and bring speakers and events to campus.

> **"Trying to find a person of color at Colby is like the search for rainbow marshmallows in a bowl of Lucky Charms. You spot a few falling into the bowl as you're pouring, but when you set your mind to finding as many as you can, none turn up."**

Q "**Anyone who speaks out is ostracized**, blamed for increasing student tensions, and usually have their name splattered all over the Digest of Civil Discourse, and the joke Echo."

Q "A lot of students are upper class, New England, white kids, but **Colby tries VERY hard to make a diverse campus**. The Pugh Center hosts many clubs dedicated to diversity."

Q "**Diversity is a ridiculous issue**. Colby claims to be 'diverse', and in some ways it is. For example, there are a lot of people from other countries, and there are domestic students from across the nation. But if you are thinking of diversity as only skin color, you are not going to find a very broad range at Colby."

Q "Diversity's a funny thing—I never think of it unless someone brings it up (which is strange since I applied here as a minority.) Colby has a reasonable amount of diversity, but more wouldn't hurt. **Colby is making a strong effort to diversify**, though."

Q "The administration puts a big emphasis on diversity, but I don't think there is enough. A few **too many rich white kids who have no idea about the rest of the world** go here."

Q "I'm from Maine, and **it's great to meet so many different people**. I have friends from California, Colorado, New York, Missouri, Wisconsin, North Carolina and Kansas, as well as foreign countries like Ghana and Germany. On the other hand, I have a lot of friends from Massachusetts and Connecticut as well."

Q "**Ubiquitous international students add fascinating perspectives**. You can join in debates over lunch about politics in Zimbabwe."

Q "The college tries, as do its NESCAC counterparts, to pretend that we are diverse. **The population is mainly white**, upper-to-middle class, and dressed in J. Crew."

Q "This is one area where Colby is lacking. **The majority of Colby students are rich, white kids from New England** who drive SUV's and wear a lot of J. Crew and Polo."

Q "**Colby is diverse by Maine standards**, but there is a definite rift between the minority groups, and the privileged white kids on campus."

The College Prowler Take On...
Diversity

We have a large population of international students, and minorities are very vocal. The campus is pretty polarized between the activist types and the non-political kids. The Foss/Mary Low side of campus tends to be more politically aware and diverse, or at least more aware of diversity. Social class has been a particular topic of concern lately—many people see Colby as very elitist. All these diversity related issues, though, are pretty actively brought to light. We've had a racial awareness week and a social class awareness week, both of which have featured lectures, discussions, and (most visibly) chalkings on the pathways. There is, though, definitely a typical "Colby kid"—Boston or New York born and bred, went to a prep school, wears polo shirts with the collars up and flip flops year-round. But the minority is very vocal, and the collars-up crowd has a very good sense of humor about their own position.

Although the campus is working very hard to create a more diverse atmosphere, and although questions of diversity are brought to light by vocal minorities and activists, the general campus attitude is largely apathetic. Minorities continue to feel marginalized, and the people who speak out on their behalf often end up feeling ostracized as well. This creates a pretty intense atmosphere sometimes—discussions and demonstrations can feel pretty heated at times. But continual efforts to introduce more diversity and alleviate tensions are definitely to be applauded.

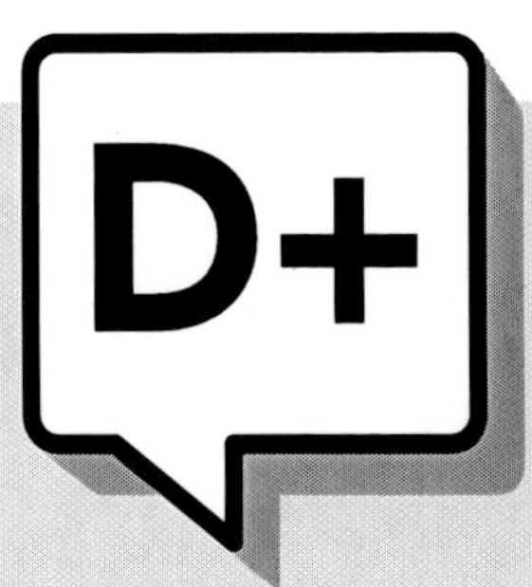

The College Prowler™ Grade on

Diversity: D+

A high grade in Diversity indicates that ethnic minorities and international students have a notable presence on campus and that students of different economic backgrounds, religious beliefs, and sexual preferences are well-represented.

The Lowdown On...
Guys & Girls

Men Undergrads:
817

Women Undergrads:
951

Birth Control Available?
Yes, for $10 per pack at the Garrison-Foster Health Center.

Hookups or Relationships?
Either/or, but casual dating is almost unheard of. Colby students tend to either hook up very randomly and very frequently, or get involved in intense and long-term relationships.

Best Place to Meet Guys/Girls:

Hookups tend to begin in classes—no, that's a joke. The party scene at Colby is where the hookup-style relationships grow and flourish (and flourish they do). Alcohol is a pretty prominent aspect of life on the Hill—it's not at all uncommon to come across students gathered in dorm rooms downing Natty Light on a Tuesday night. Head to any of the established party dorm (Dana, Foss, Heights, and AMS are notable), grab a can of beer, and watch the world of college hookups unfold. Heights dances are especially famous, as one student said, "I hope to God there's an entire chapter devoted to Heights dances in this book." Relationships that begin under these alcohol-induced situations tend to measure their longevity in minutes or hours, maybe days if the hookup lasts through the weekend.

Looking for a relationship? Real life at Colby (as opposed to the party world) revolves around classes and dorms, making these the best places to find true love (or at least a more substantial relationship). Small class sizes and after-hours study sessions make the academics at Colby great, but they also make it a lot easier to get to know that hot guy/girl in the back row. Getting to know the people in your building, or in the buildings of friends, can help spark relationships, too. There's nothing like complaining about the crowded laundry rooms to develop a sentimental bond. Dining halls are good places to meet people as well. Colby students are noted for their friendliness, so it's not at all uncommon to strike up a conversation with the beautiful stranger standing behind you in the omelet line.

Did You Know?
Top Places to Find Hotties:
1. Facebook

2. Dances (especially in Heights)

3. Off-campus parties

Top Places to Hookup:

1. Dances (especially in Heights)
2. Any dorm elevator
3. Practice rooms in Bixler
4. Miller Library
5. The laundry rooms

Dress Code

"Collars up" is practically a mantra at Colby. The typical Colby student wears khakis or Nantucket reds, a polo shirt with an upturned collar (two, in complimentary pastels, to be really trendy), and flip-flops. Girls accessorize with **pearls and hair-ribbons,** guys might pull out a **hemp or shell necklace.** Nalgenes are key. Decorated with stickers proclaiming a love of Guster, skiing, or both.

Guys & Girls

> **"I feel that the Colby students are generally attractive. The dating scene is interesting. You are either dating (which means you are practically married) or you are just hooking up. It is very hard to find an in between."**

Q "Colby is known for its **beautiful people**."

Q "**Most people here are very nice**, even though they dress preppy."

Q "One can find pretty attractive women and pretty loud and annoying girls. **Colby has an on-line dating service called "Mulematch"**—use it at your discretion."

Q "**People are mostly friendly**, rich and white, but that's not their fault."

Q "I chose Colby because it had the most **friendly, welcoming atmosphere** of any school I visited. After attending Colby for two years, it hasn't changed."

Q "**We have a very attractive campus**. Everyone is so friendly; I was struck when I first came here that everyone smiled at you, even if you didn't know who they were. Although, all the Ralph Lauren, Tiffany's heart bracelets, and pastel matching seemed a little over–the-top."

Q "**There are some hotties**—no doubt."

Q "Both sexes are very down to earth and chill. **Colby people are so easy to get along with**."

Q "**Walking around Colby is a little like walking into a J. Crew catalogue**. Upturned collars, Northface and Patagonia fleece, and a good, healthy dose of preppiness are the general atmosphere. We've also got a handful of hippies, but punks are rarely seen on Mayflower Hill."

Q "Guys tend to be sophomoric and moronic socially despite how intelligent they are. Their potential starts to show senior year, but until then they act like idiots. Most Colby girls, despite how shallow or ignorant they can seem, are overall smart and sweet. All you have to do is spend five minutes talking with them and you'll see that there's gold in them all. And **the girls are hot, plain and simple**."

Q "The best way to get a handle on some standout Colby personalities is to **open up the daily digest**."

Q "Enrollment at Colby College is **contingent on being a sexy beast**."

Q "**I think the girls are much more attractive than the boys**. Many of the girls are 'naturally pretty' and do not try to emulate Britney Spears. For the most part, they dress on the more conservative side and in a respectable manner. I think that it is difficult to meet guys on this campus. You can meet people at parties, but I wish there was some other type of social interaction during the week where people could meet on sober terms."

Q "**Colby is a good looking campus** with a wide range of personalities."

The College Prowler Take On...
Guys & Girls

Most people choose to come to Colby because of the friendliness of the students. Colby folks smile at each other, make conversation easily, and are typically overwhelmingly optimistic. Alcohol is definitely a huge part of the social scene, though, and can get to be a bit much at times. Great chem.-free living is very important for people who aren't into the drinking scene. Work-hard, play-hard is a term practically modeled off social life at Colby. Classes are rigorous and homework does pile up, but for most students, weekends are sacrosanct. Many take partying almost as seriously as they take their studies, discussing pre-game techniques avidly before class.

Although the populace is, in general, preppy or crunchy/hippie, everyone tends to be accepting and friendly. Expect to wave to or smile at most of the people you pass as you walk from the dining hall to the library, and be prepared to meet and converse with too many people to remember during the first weeks of school. The small campus means you get to know people very quickly. This is good and bad—if you develop a reputation you can easily be ostracized, and there are definitely cliques. They might smile at each other and talk during class, but you'll rarely see the activist kids at the same parties as the jocks on the weekends (or during the week).

The College Prowler™ Grade on

Guys: C+

A high grade for Guys indicates that the male population on campus is attractive, smart, friendly, and engaging, and that the school has a decent ratio of guys to girls.

The College Prowler™ Grade on

Girls: B+

A high grade for Girls not only implies that the women on campus are attractive, smart, friendly, and engaging, but also that there is a fair ratio of girls to guys.

Athletics

The Lowdown On...
Athletics

Athletic Division:
NCAA Division III

Conference:
NESCAC

Men's Varsity Sports:
Cross Country Track
Football
Golf
Soccer
Alpine Skiing
Basketball
Hockey
Indoor Track
Nordic Skiing
Skiing
Baseball
Crew
Lacrosse
Outdoor Track
Tennis

Women's Varsity Sports:

Cross Country

Field Hockey

Golf

Soccer

Volleyball

Alpine Skiing

Basketball

Ice Hockey

Indoor Track

Nordic Skiing

Swimming

Crew

Lacrosse

Outdoor Track

Softball

Tennis

Club Sports:

Ballroom Dance

Badminton

Cheer Club

Cycling Club

Equestrians

Fencing

Rugby (men's and women's)

Tai Chi Julebu

Men's Volleyball

Sailing

Ultimate Frisbee

Woodsmen's Team (co-ed; this involves axes and chainsaws)

Intramurals:

Field Hockey

Soccer (competitive and recreational)

Flag Football (competitive and recreational)

Broomball

Basketball (5-on-5 and 3-on-3)

Triathlon

Home Run Derby

Softball (competitive and recreational

Athletic Fields

Synthetic track, fifty acres of fields (includes football, soccer, and lacrosse), ten tennis courts, cross-country running and ski trails and a lumberjack area..

School Mascot

A white mule. This mascot originated in 1923, when Colby students decided they were tired of being referred to as the dark horse competitors in athletics.

Getting Tickets

Is not a problem. The football game against Bates, and the hockey game against Bowdoin are well attended, but crowds don't tend to grace Colby's fields.

Most Popular Sports

Hockey, Lacrosse, Broomball, Ultimate Frisbee, Campus Golf (not a real sport, but very popular regardless)

Overlooked Teams

Football, Badminton, Squash, Rugby

Best Place to Take a Walk

Colby-Hume Center, the wooded trails behind the athletic center

Gyms/Facilities

Harold Alfond Athletic Center: the only gym on campus. It houses a twenty-five-yard by twenty-five-meter pool, an ice rink for ice hockey and broomball, an indoor track and indoor tennis courts, two basketball courts, a weight-training center, squash courts, and aerobics room, saunas, a climbing wall, and a training and physical therapy center. The weight room can get crowded after classes get out, and most people don't even know the saunas exist, but kickboxing and yoga classes in the aerobics room are well attended and the ice rink gets a good deal of use.

Number of Males Playing Varsity Sports:

305

Percent of Males Playing Varsity Sports:

36%

Number of Females Playing Varsity Sports:

302

Percent of Females Playing Varsity Sports:

31%

> **"Because Colby is so small, sometimes it feels as though almost everyone plays a sport, whether varsity or club. Colby is a very athletic and outdoorsy school—most students are active in some way."**

Q "**The majority of campus is involved in sports** (either intramural or varsity). If you are not a member of a team most exercise and stay active on their own."

Q "The campus is very active, but that means everything from gym, to varsity sports, to skiing, to hiking, all depending on the weather. **The skiing and crew teams are good**, but the other teams don't really match up to the schools we compete against. Intramural teams are popular and really fun."

Q "Varsity sports are very popular, but not enough people watch the games. **Intramural sports are very popular and are so much fun**. Everybody plays broomball—it's the most fun you'll ever have getting the crap kicked out of yourself."

Q "There's a significant group that plays varsity sports, but an equally significant one that doesn't. The interaction between these groups is fairly good. If you play a varsity sport, there's a strong tendency to get sucked in and have few friends outside the team, though. **Intramural sports are popular**. Not everyone wants to play sports, but for those who do, there's a sport and a level for anyone."

Q **"Varsity sports are pretty big**, but if you are used to a big crowd at football games you are not going to find it at Colby. You will get to know a lot of the players, so it's fun to watch your friends. Intramural is really big. I have played soccer and softball recreationally, but you can also play competitively."

Q **"Sports are big**, but they aren't everything."

Q "Varsity sports are pretty big and **intramural sports are really fun**—Go Mules!"

Q "The student body can be easily excited by school rivalries. **The Colby-Bates football game and the Colby-Bowdoin hockey game are famous**. Around the time of the Colby-Bates football game, you see many students wearing 'Buck Fates' tee-shirts."

Q "A lot of people are on varsity sports teams, and they definitely create their own circles of friends through those teams, but it's nothing like a big sports school where sports are the only social life on campus. IM sports are pretty popular, and they have both recreational and competitive leagues. **Broomball is probably the most fun**—it involves sliding around the hockey rink trying to hit a ball with a broom-like stick."

The College Prowler Take On...
Athletics

Colby is definitely not famous for its athletic prowess. "Real" sports don't get too much attention here, certainly not as much as they do at major universities with big football teams. Lacrosse and soccer can be pretty popular, and hockey games are comparatively well attended. The Bates football rivalry and the Bowdoin hockey rivalry boost the attendance at those games, as well. But, despite the lack of emphasis on varsity sports, Colby students are outdoorsy and athletic. Lots of people ski and snowboard in the winter, and sledding down the Lorimer Chapel hill on stolen cafeteria trays is always fun. Ultimate Frisbee and broomball (which is like ice hockey, except you wear sneakers instead of skates, and use a mini-soccer ball instead of a puck) are the most played sports. The intramural teams, known as I-play sports, are more popular than the varsity sports, and are a great way to get to know people outside of your dorm and your classes.

Although varsity sports do not define life at Colby, students are far from lazy armchair-dwellers. I-Play sports are fun and casual, you can even choose to play recreationally rather than competitively on most teams. January is a great time for winter athletes – the relaxed nature of Jan-plan provides lots of time to drive to Sugarloaf Mountain and ski or snowboard. Most students stay active without getting competitive.

The College Prowler™ Grade on
Athletics: C+

A high grade in Athletics indicates that students have school spirit, that sports programs are respected, that games are well-attended, and that intramurals are a prominent part of student life.

Nightlife

The Lowdown On...
Nightlife

Club and Bar Prowler: Popular Nightlife Spots!

Although it appears as though a club or two exists in Waterville, students tend to get their kicks at the on-campus Heights dances or off-campus parties.

Champion's
30 Elm Plaza, Waterville
Phone: (207) 873 - 0571

Clem's Place
40 College Ave, Waterville
Phone: (207) 872-9864

Pete and Larry's Lounge
375 Upper Main Street, Waterville
Phone: (207) 873-0111

Spirits Tavern
6 Elm Plaza, Waterville
Phone: (207) 873-0571

The Bob-In, Bootleggers, Mainely Brews and Spirits are pretty well attended. Some of them will have senior nights, which adds to their popularity. They all require driving, though, so many will frequent the on-campus pub to avoid having to pay cab fare.

The Bob-In

(17 Temple Street, Waterville
Phone: (207) 873-5842

Bootleggers Tavern

26 Elm St., Waterville
Phone: (207) 872-4949

Mainely Brews Tavern

1 Post Office Square, Waterville
Phone: (207) 873-2457

Safari Bar

14 Silver Street, Waterville
Phone: (207) 873-2277

Spirits

2 Silver St., Waterville
Phone: (207) 877-8990

Spotter's Restaurant and Pub

155 West River Road, Waterville
Phone: (207) 873-2277

You Know Whose Pub

The Concourse, Waterville
Phone: (207) 873-5255

Bars Close At:

1-2 a.m.

Student Favorites:

Mainely Brews, The Bob-In, Bootlegger's, You Know Whose

Cheapest Place to Get a Drink:

The Pub. If you're a cute girl, just wander around Dana on the weekends.

Local Specialties:

Mule Juice. And Orloff Vodka is brewed nearby.

Useful Resources for Nightlife:

Upperclassmen, www.thomas.edu/GENINFO/dining

What to Do if You're Not 21

Again, just wander around the dorms. Don't try to get into the Pub, because they're good at spotting fakes. Upperclassmen are usually more than willing to help an under-twenty-one-er in need—getting alcohol doesn't tend to be a problem.

Organization Parties:

Some sports teams will throw themselves parties, which usually consist of too many bottles of Mad Dog in the woods before dinner. Outsiders are very much not invited to these shindigs, but if you see exceptionally drunk athletes stumbling toward a dining hall, you can pretty much assume it was a sports party. Cast parties for student performances tend to be just as loud, but usually take place in a big dorm room or the senior apartments, and are therefore slightly less obvious.

Favorite Drinking Games:

Beer Die (a Colby creation)

Beirut

Frats

See the Greek Section!

Nightlife

"The main party scene is off campus. There are a lot of off-campus houses with names like 'the Lodge' and 'Paradise' that upperclassmen live in, and they throw the best parties."

Q "While you can almost **always find a party on campus**, in recent years the off-campus party scene has increased. Students generally pre-party in dorm rooms before heading off campus to upperclassmen houses or local bars. Mainely Brews is especially popular."

Q "Parties are **awesome**, but can get old at times."

Q "Parties on campus can be described in two words— **excessive drinking.**"

Q "The **parties on campus are always great.** If you want, you can find several pretty much every weekend. True, most of them are just a lot of drinking, but every one I've been to has been really open to getting something else started."

Q "People party to celebrate the weekend. **It gets a bit repetitive** after awhile."

Q "The party scene is **inclusive, fun, and largely reliant on alcohol.**"

Q "The **parties are a lot of fun**—I'm not going to deny it. At Colby we like the work hard, play hard ethic. Sometimes the drinking atmosphere is a little forced, but people are usually good about not pressuring you to drink if you don't want to."

Q "Parties on campus are pretty good. SPB (the Student Programming Board) hosts events every weekend, and **many people organize their own shindigs as well.** Off-campus partying seems to be growing in popularity—you can usually find that one of the upper-classmen living off-campus is hosting a party at some point during the weekend."

Q "**Parties are generally on campus and in dorms.** The school SPB parties are pretty awesome because people really go. Off-campus parties are so hard to get to, but parties on campus are fun because we're allowed to drink in the dorms and anyone can come."

Q "The dorm parties are just like any other party—**drinking, socializing, and maybe some dancing.** School-sponsored parties are usually dances that start at 8 or 9 p.m. and end at 1 a.m."

Q "The pub on campus is only for students over twenty-one, and they're pretty strict about that. **Parties tend to be kind of low key** (just friends in rooms and stuff) if you stay on campus. Dances can be fun if people go. If you're on campus, you need to watch out, and not get an open-container fine, because the campus is cracking down on drinking and partying. There are always good off-campus parties."

Q "Bars and clubs off-campus are almost non-existent. **There are no clubs—let's be honest, it's central Maine.** There are a couple of bars that do become popular once you are twenty-one, or a senior—they often sponsor senior nights, but underclassmen tend to stay on campus or go to off-campus houses to party. In the past couple of years security has become a lot more rigid about breaking up parties on campus, which is pushing people to off-campus houses for partying. This is unfortunate, as the campus party life used to be the center of social life, and a lot of fun."

Q "Life at Colby tends to revolve around alcohol. **School events without alcohol are generally poorly attended,** and alcohol-free parties are generally abandoned early in the night in favor of alcoholic ones."

The College Prowler Take On...
Nightlife

Small parties that can fit into dorm rooms without arousing too much suspicion from security are abundant on campus. These parties usually consist of a bunch of friends drinking, listening to music, and breaking out their stolen Colby tables for games of beer die or Beirut. The Blue Light Pub is always busy, but you can only get in if you're over twenty-one, and they are very, very good at spotting fake ids. Huge parties happen almost every weekend at off-campus houses, and bars and nightclubs are a good alternative to the routine on-campus drinking. Security has gotten tighter about busting unregistered parties. There is a party host system, which means that trained party hosts can have lots of people, and alcohol in their room without getting in trouble, but it's an unpaid, and very risky, position, so registered parties are few and far between.

There is always something to do on campus. Usually there are concerts or performances, followed by countless on-campus parties. It's common to 'pre-game' at a smaller on-campus party, then hop in a cab, and drink the night away at the bigger off-campus scene. Students over twenty-one who live on campus will visit the Pub; the ones who live off-campus find it easier to frequent the bars and taverns of Waterville. There is little variety. Once you've established a party pattern (are you an off-campus partier? A light, on-campus drinker? A social butterfly, flitting from room to room?), you tend to stick to it. And alcohol is an important part of the experience. You can choose not to drink, and no one will hassle you too much, but even the chem.-free students tend to end up sipping something by the end of the night.

The College Prowler™ Grade on

Nightlife: B-

A high grade in Nightlife indicates that there are many bars and clubs in the area that are easily accessible and affordable. Other determining factors include the number of options for the under-21 crowd and the prevalence of house parties.

Greek Life

The Lowdown On...
Greek Life

Number of Fraternities:
0

Number of Sororities:
0

Students Speak Out On...
Greek Life

> **"There are rumors of secret frats at Colby, but if the rumors are true no one is speaking up about them. Some swear the secret frats exist; others claim they're nothing but Colby legend. "**

Q "Ha! There's **no Greek life at Colby!**"

Q "I like that there's no Greek life at Colby. **Everyone does their own thing** and nobody thinks that they're better than anyone else. Sure, there are cliques, but for the most part, everyone's pretty laid back."

Q "I kind of wish there was a cool frat house on campus. Then **we'd actually have something to do** on the weekends!"

Q "No Greek life at all. **I'm not complaining!**"

Q "I'm glad there are no frats at Colby. **The Olympics are fun,** though, and give us a chance to get drunk and act like a bunch of frat kids. Once a year isn't bad!"

Q "Seriously, the campus is a lot better off without frats. Everyone does their own thing and it's a lot more fun for everyone. Frats tend to form cliques that single people out as 'cool,' and 'not cool.' **Colby is for everyone.** Not just the cool kids."

The College Prowler Take On...
Greek Life

Don't come to Colby looking to pledge or hook-up with a frat boy. Fraternities and sororities were abolished in 1984, because they were associated with excessive drinking, segregation, hazing, and sexual assault. They made certain groups of people very uncomfortable while they existed (especially women and minorities). Currently there has been heated debate about establishing multicultural housing. Many people think that establishing multicultural housing will take Colby back to the days of exclusion and separatism. Others say that problems of discrimination were not felled by the banning of Greek life, and multicultural housing is intended to remedy problems of discrimination.

Most students seem to think the abolishment of frats was a positive development. They simply weren't working with the small size and isolated atmosphere of Colby College . The party scene has survived the abolition pretty much intact, especially in the dorms that used to be frat houses. They are still referred to as the frat row dorms (despite the administration's insistence on calling it Robert's Row). The frat-row Olympics in the fall reclaims the fraternity traditions in an inclusive and good-heartedly competitive way.

The College Prowler™ Grade on
Greek Life: N/A

A high grade in Greek Life indicates that sororities and fraternities are not only present, but also active on campus. Other determining factors include the variety of houses available and the respect the Greek community receives from the rest of the campus.

Drug Scene

The Lowdown On...
Drug Scene

Most Prevalent Drugs on Campus:

- Marijuana
- Study drugs
(Ritalin and Adderall, for example)

Liquor-Related Referrals:
0

Liquor-Related Arrests:
15

Drug-Related Referrals:
0

Drug-Related Arrests:
0

Drug Counseling Programs

Maine General Hospital Substance Abuse Services

Phone: (207) 872-4140

Services: Emergency services, inpatient treatment, partial hospitalization, outpatient services, intensive outpatient day and evening services, adolescent services

Substance Counselor, Rachel Henderson

Phone: (207) 872-3394

Services: confidential counseling and evaluations

Students Speak Out On...
Drug Scene

"There are drugs, but they're not widely used. When they are, it's not in the open."

Q "When it comes time to turn papers in, **kids stick a bunch of Ritalin up their noses** and turn things in on extension."

Q "Basically just '**Mary the Iguana**'."

Q "The illegal drug scene is overall weak and deep underground. **Everyone knows someone who smokes pot**, and someone else who smokes up all the time, but no one will try to pressure you to. Alcohol is everywhere. It's rare for there to be pressure to drink, but it does happen. Binge drinking is really common."

Q "Drugs are **not all over the place**."

Q "**There is a lot of pot**, but if you are not into it no one cares one way or the other. You can easily have fun without it. There are more hardcore drugs scattered around, but I have never come in contact with them."

Q "**The only fun drugs you can easily obtain are marijuana and ADD medication**. Sadly, prescription meds are difficult to come by, and I have not yet seen cocaine. If this is what you are looking for, try a city university."

Q "If you want it, **you can find it**."

 www.collegeprowler.com

Q "**Colby kids do love their weed**, but besides that drugs are not a huge presence on campus."

Q "**Drugs are there**, but aren't dominant."

Q "There are a good number of pot smokers and not much else. **Most people just drink**."

The College Prowler Take On...
Drug Scene

There is no cocaine in the bathrooms for Colby students. We may be reliant on alcohol for fun, but drug use is rare and kept quiet. Marijuana is the biggest illicit vice; certain dorms never really lose that stoner smell. Hard drug use does exist, and those who are looking for drugs know where to find them. Almost everyone has heard tales of the local tattoo and piercing parlor, where the piercing artists deal coke and heroine on their days off, but you would have to be actively looking for drugs to come in contact with them. Study drugs can be a problem, though. People who are on prescription attention drugs have had problems with friends or acquaintances looking to buy their medicine for an extra paper-writing boost.

Too much time listening to Phish may have led some Colby students to smoke marijuana, and intense academics can push some people to seek illegal study drugs. Neither of these ever seems like a real threat, though. Harder drugs are practically non-existent, so the campus tends to feel very safe from illicit chemical activity. Oh and don't forget about alcohol—yes, it is a drug, and it seems to be the drug of choice, so the drug scene is probably no different than any other school.

The College Prowler™ Grade on

Drug Scene: B+

A high grade in the Drug Scene indicates that drugs are not a noticeable part of campus life; drug use is not visible, and no pressure to use them seems to exist.

www.collegeprowler.com

Campus Strictness

The Lowdown On...
Campus Strictness

What Are You Most Likely to Get Caught Doing on Campus?

- Drinking alcohol from an open container in the hallways
- Underage drinking
- Having too many people in a dorm room
- Illegally possessing a Colby table (frequently stolen as Beer Die or Beirut tables)
- Making too much noise during quiet hours
- Propping doors open

> **"A lot of people say security is too strict; I say they aren't strict enough. One time I was working in Miller Library, and I had to clean up beer bottles left over by drunken students."**

Q "**Secrity is strict enough to keep the campus safe**, but flexible enough to allow for some fun over the weekends."

Q "**Things are getting stricter**, but we are still much cooler than other schools."

Q "**I wouldn't be caught with a beer in my hand** and security in sight."

Q "**Security is not very strict at all**. Underclassmen can even get alcohol without much of a problem. The only violation you'll get is having an open container in a non-approved area."

Q "Sometimes you can have a loud party that will last until the morning, but other times campus security will be rapping at the door just an hour into it. **It seems to vary nightly.**"

Q "**They are becoming much more strict** about the drinking, and this is pissing off the student body. People still manage to party, but the number of complaints are growing."

Q "Campus security has been tightening up recently, and coming up with more consequences for getting caught. **There is a very strict open-container policy** with a hefty fine, and there is also a strict underage drinking fine. As long as you stay in your room, keep the door closed, and turn the music down, you'll be fine."

Q "In the chem.-free dorms you get kicked out if you are caught with alcohol or drugs, and **the drug policy is stricter than the alcohol policy**, but neither merits immediate expulsion."

Q "**Security is pretty strict about drinking**, but is much more relaxed than many other schools I visited."

Q "**If security decides to bust you, you're not going to get out if it.** They usually give pretty fair warning for drinking though. I've seen them standing in the hallway outside a party not doing anything, just reminding students of their job. As long as the party you're at isn't busted they won't do anything about you if you're underage and drunk. They're really strict about the open container policy, though. No one, regardless of age, can have open alcohol outside of the place where they got it. Basically security gives a pretty wide berth, but there is a definite line, and you don't want to even try to walk it."

The College Prowler Take On...
Campus Strictness

Colby does seem to be getting stricter about drinking and partying. While the administrative take on partying is pretty much: students are going to drink and party, so we should make sure they don't end up in the hospital or in jail. However, to avoid getting in trouble with the police, hefty open container fines have added to the strictness of security. Don't walk around the halls with an open can of beer; you're pretty much asking for trouble. Strictness can vary from dorm-to-dorm, or from night-to-night, as well. Every dorm has Head Residents (HRs) who make sure no one has died in the bathrooms on weekend nights, and can issue citations and call security if parties get too loud or raucous. Some HRs will be more lenient than others. Some security guards, too, are stricter. Most people know at least one security guard fairly well, which is a good way to avoid getting a citation.

Most students think that security has gotten tighter on campus, especially with regards to partying and drinking. It has become more difficult to have huge parties on campus, and increased harshness has led to a bigger off-campus party scene. But most agree that, especially in comparison to friend's schools, Colby students are pretty lucky.

The College Prowler™ Grade on

Campus Strictness: C-

A high Campus Strictness grade implies an overall lenient atmosphere; police and RAs are fairly tolerant, and the administration's rules are flexible.

Parking

The Lowdown On...
Parking

Parking Permit Cost
Free

Colby Parking Services:
Office of Security
(207) 872-3345
bamcdoug@colby.edu
www.colby.edu/personnel/security/parking

Student Parking Lot?
Three

Freshman Allowed to Park?
Yes

Parking Permits

The Department of Security issues parking permits for free, although they limit one permit per person.

Did You Know?

Best Places to Find a Parking Spot

The Bob's lot always has spots, although you might have to walk a bit.

Good Luck Getting a Parking Spot Here!

The coveted first tier of the Hillside lot.

"Parking is sometimes a pain since you are allowed to bring a car all four years. This usually just means you have to park in a lot that is farther away from your dorm. And when you think about it, you never have to walk more than ten minutes, because Colby is so small."

Q "It's very **easy to park** on campus."

Q "It wasn't so bad to park at the beginning of the year, but with new construction projects that have eliminated some spaces, **it's getting harder to find spots**, especially late at night."

Q "**Parking is not too bad**, especially compared to other schools. It's annoying when you have to park in snow banks and dig out your car the next morning."

Q "Luckily at Colby all students are allowed to have a car. In my opinion, this should be restricted to upperclassmen because it is often difficult to find a space late at night, but I can't complain because **having a car is a huge convenience**."

Q "**It can get crowded**, but it's reasonable enough."

Q "**There are enough parking lots on campus**, but you will most likely be pretty far from your dorm."

Q "None of the people I knew who had a car had **any trouble with parking.**"

Q "Does your car have **a good turning radius?**"

Q "**Parking can be tricky.** Be prepared to walk a bit to get to your car."

Q "Parking: **really easy.**"

Q "**There's plenty of parking for all years**—even for freshmen."

All students are allowed to park, and those who park in the Bobs or Foss lots tend to find it very easy. The biggest complaint there is the snow. It's awful to be snowed in under the best of circumstances, but the snowplows create snow banks that can make getting a car out of the parking lot nearly impossible. Students who park behind Hillside have an extra challenge—bad parkers and a very poorly designed tiered lot. The lines are worn away, and students tend to have an uncanny ability to take up two spaces. And if you can't find a spot on the first tier, you have to back out to get to the second tier—still no dice? Put 'er in reverse and try the third or fourth tiers—Good luck.

It's easy (and valid) to complain about the Hillside parking. In general, though, the parking at Colby is pretty easy. All students can have cars, which is great—even freshman can have cars on campus, which is unusual on quite a few college campuses, so there should not be a high volume of complaints. Campus is far enough from town that having a car is very helpful, especially during the cold winters. Parking spots are always available, although it might be a long walk back to the dorm.

The College Prowler™ Grade on

Parking: B-

A high grade in this section indicates that parking is both available and affordable, and that parking enforcement isn't overly severe.

Transportation

The Lowdown On...
Transportation

Ways to Get Around Town

On Campus

Security escort: 24 hours with a phone call

Jitney: 2 p.m. –12 a.m. Sunday-Wednesday, 2 p.m.- 2 a.m. Thursday-Saturday; runs on a schedule until 6 p.m. and after that by request

Public Transportation

Jitney: 2 p.m. –12 a.m. Sunday-Wednesday, 2 p.m.- 2 a.m. Thursday-Saturday; runs on a schedule until 6 p.m. and after that by request.

Taxi Cabs

Elm City Cab
(207) 872-0101

Elite Taxi
(207) 872-2221

Car Rentals

Avis
local: (207) 874-7500;
national: (800) 831-2847
www.avis.com

Budget
local: (207) 873-1188;
national: (800) 527-0700
www.budget.com

Enterprise
local: (207) 877-6601;
national: (800) 736-8222
www.enterprise.com

Car Rentals (*Continued...*)

Hertz
local: (207) 774-4544;
national: (800) 654-3131
www.hertz.com

National
local: (207) 773-0036;
national: (800) 227-7368
www.nationalcar.com

Best Ways to Get Around Town

Start begging your parents for a car.

Before you make friends with someone or start dating someone, ask yourself: "do they have a car? Will they let me borrow it?"

When it's nice out you can walk or ride a bike into town. But it's not often nice out.

Ways to Get Out of Town
Airlines Serving Portland:

American Airlines, (800) 433-7300, www.americanairlines.com

Continental, (800) 525-0280, www.continental.com

Delta, (800) 221-1212, www.delta-air.com

Northwest, (800) 225-2525, www.nwa.com

United Express, (800) 241-6522, www.united.com

US Airways, (800) 428-4322, www.usairways.com

Airport

Portland International Jetport, (207) 879-1903

At 78 miles away, the Portland Jetport is about an hour and a half drive from Colby

How to Get There

Colby subsidizes airport shuttles for enrolled students, so we only have to pay half prices. During busy times, like holidays, you can almost always get a good group rate. Parents can use these same shuttle services at full price.

Classy Limo, (800) 499-0663
Mermaid Transportation, (800) 696-2463
Excalibur Limousine Service, (800) 317-8256
Northeast Charter and Tour, (888) 593-6328

Greyhound

There is a Vermont Transit/Greyhound bus terminal about two miles from campus. Call (800) 231-2222 for schedules.

Amtrak

There's an Amtrak station in Portland – an hour and a half drive from campus. Call (800) 872-7245 for schedules.

Portland Amtrak Train Station

Portland Transportation Center
100 Sewall St.
Portland, ME 04102
(207) 828-3939

Travel Agents

Hewins Travel, 135 Main Street,
Waterville
(207) 364-3792

Students Speak Out On...
Transportation

"Public transportation is pretty convenient. Not enough people take advantage of the transportation that the school provides, like the Jitney."

Q "The **Jitney is convenient**."

Q "The town itself does not have any public transportation, but **Colby runs a Jitney service**, which goes into town at certain hours, and will pick you up again later. You can also call the Jitney at any time of the day to have them drive you around, although getting back to campus can sometimes involve an annoying wait."

Q "Public transportation kind of sucks. The Jitney is hard to use—**you're better off getting a friend to take you into town**."

Q "Oh, the **Jitney**…"

Q "The taxi service is pretty reliable but it gets expensive. **The Jitney is free**, but you're going to have to wait a while. Every time I've used it I've been stuck in town for an hour after I call for it. I would suggest that if you want to get into town, find someone with a car, and ask if they want to go or if you can borrow it."

Q "There's a student-run service called the Jitney. It's not very convenient because it takes a while for them to come after you've called them. **I suggest getting a ride or having a car on campus**."

Q **"The Jitney service is really bad**. The drivers are mostly rude, often miss work, and the hours and pick-ups are inconvenient. You don't need a car, but if you'd like to move about Waterville it helps a whole lot."

Q "The Jitney seems like it's **rarely running**."

Q **"The Jitney can get you where you want to go**, but the key word is patience."

Q **"Forty dollars for a bus ride to Boston** is a disgrace to the nation."

Q "The bus stop is **only a mile or two from campus**."

The College Prowler Take On...
Transportation

Until they perfect the art of molecular beaming, there's not much hope for isolated Colby students. The single most effective way to get around Waterville, Maine, or New England is to have a car or make friends with someone who does. Fortunately for Colby students, everyone is allowed to have a car on campus, so finding transportation isn't nearly as hard as it could be. Colby does have a student-run shuttle called the Jitney. An overwhelming majority of students think of the Jitney as unreliable and difficult to use, though. The security office has taxi-vouchers, but these are not often used, either. In fact, some of the taxi services don't even accept the vouchers any more. Colby subsidizes shuttles to the airport, although the least expensive service was recently unable to produce proof of insurance, and is no longer available. The Amtrak Downeaster is a great way to get to Boston and New York, and is relatively inexpensive, but it still takes an hour and a half to get to the Portland Amtrak station.

It's possible to get off campus without a car, but it's also expensive and sometimes unreliable. If you have a car, bring it. If you don't, don't worry too much because you'll almost assuredly be friends with someone who does. But don't count on public transportation to get you around.

The College Prowler™ Grade on
Transportation: D

A high grade for Transportation indicates that campus buses, public buses, cabs, and rental cars are readily-available and affordable. Other determining factors include proximity to an airport and the necessity of transportation.

Weather

The Lowdown On...
Weather

Average Temperature		Average Precipitation	
Fall:	52°F	Fall:	3.7 in.
Winter:	30 °F	Winter:	3.23 in.
Spring:	48 °F	Spring:	3.48 in.
Summer:	66 °F	Summer:	3.57 in.

Weather

"Have you ever watched the Discovery Channel specials on polar bears? If you can invest in something equivalent to their furs, do it because the temperatures are FREEZING, but once it hits forty in the spring make sure you've got you tube tops because it doesn't take much to get Colby kids back outside bearing our pale skin."

Q "Well, it is in Maine. **Expect cold and snow**; winter months can get pretty dreary, but the nice days in the spring and fall are amazing. As soon as the snow melts and the thermometer breaks thirty-two degrees you can be sure to see half the campus outside enjoying the nice weather in flip flops."

Q "It is COLD!! **January is the worst month at Colby**; we had some –50°F days. Be sure to bring lots of sweaters, warm jackets, and don't forget your polos."

Q "**Maine has incredibly harsh winters**; bring as much clothing as possible. The weather at the beginning and the end of the school year is really nice, though."

Q "**The weather can get very, very cold**, especially in January. It warms up again in May, just as the second semester is ending and finals begin."

Q "Snow like whoa—**bring lots and lots of fleece and sweaters**. If you can survive January as a freshman, you will make it through all four years."

Q **"The weather is gorgeous in the fall and the spring**. You will love the snow at the beginning, but by January you will have had enough. The school is just as fun in the winter, but come spring you will be appreciating the grass of the campus way more than you would have expected to—buy long underwear."

Q **"It's no lie that winter seems to stretch on forever**. You'll definitely need a warm jacket, and long underwear doesn't hurt either. The spring and fall are so nice, though. Once you get a spring day in the sixties, everyone is outside enjoying it."

Q "People in Maine like to talk a lot of trash about the weather, but **it's really not too bad**."

Q **"After winter you really appreciate the warm days**, and it's great to see groups of people out enjoying the weather."

Q **"Be prepared for a long, cold winter**. Lately New England has been having unusually frigid winters, and there are times when you just don't want to leave the dorm because it's so cold."

Q **"Get used to a winter that begins in early October** and ends around commencement."

Q "Bring lots of warm clothes or **you'll freeze to death—** I'm not kidding."

Q "It's freezing in January, and there is tons of wind, too. **Be prepared**."

The College Prowler Take On...
Weather

The first month of school, and the last weeks of school will be phenomenally gorgeous. The rest of the year will be bitterly cold and snowy. The good news is: you get used to it. In January the temperatures can drop into the negative fifties (counting wind chill). The campus seems to get a lot bigger in the winter, because walking to classes becomes very unpleasant. The key to surviving the harsh winter is to anticipate it. Bring lots of sweaters and thick clothing, have fun with layers, and don't get too freaked out by the concept of long underwear. A few weeks of cold weather and you'll know exactly which route will get you from your room to the dining hall in the shortest amount of time.

Colby students are optimistic, if nothing else. As soon as temperatures rise above freezing, the winter coats disappear. A few degrees warmer and the ubiquitous flip-flops begin to emerge, shortly thereafter skirts, shorts, halter-tops, and polos make an appearance. Sunny weekends are worshipped and smaller classes will often be relocated outside on nice days. These sunny weekends can be cruel jokes, especially when they happen in April and are immediately followed by a blizzard, and a sudden drop in temperature.

The College Prowler™ Grade on
Weather: C-

A high Weather grade designates that temperatures are mild and rarely reach extremes, that the campus tends to be sunny rather than rainy, and that weather is fairly consistent rather than unpredictable.

Report Card Summary

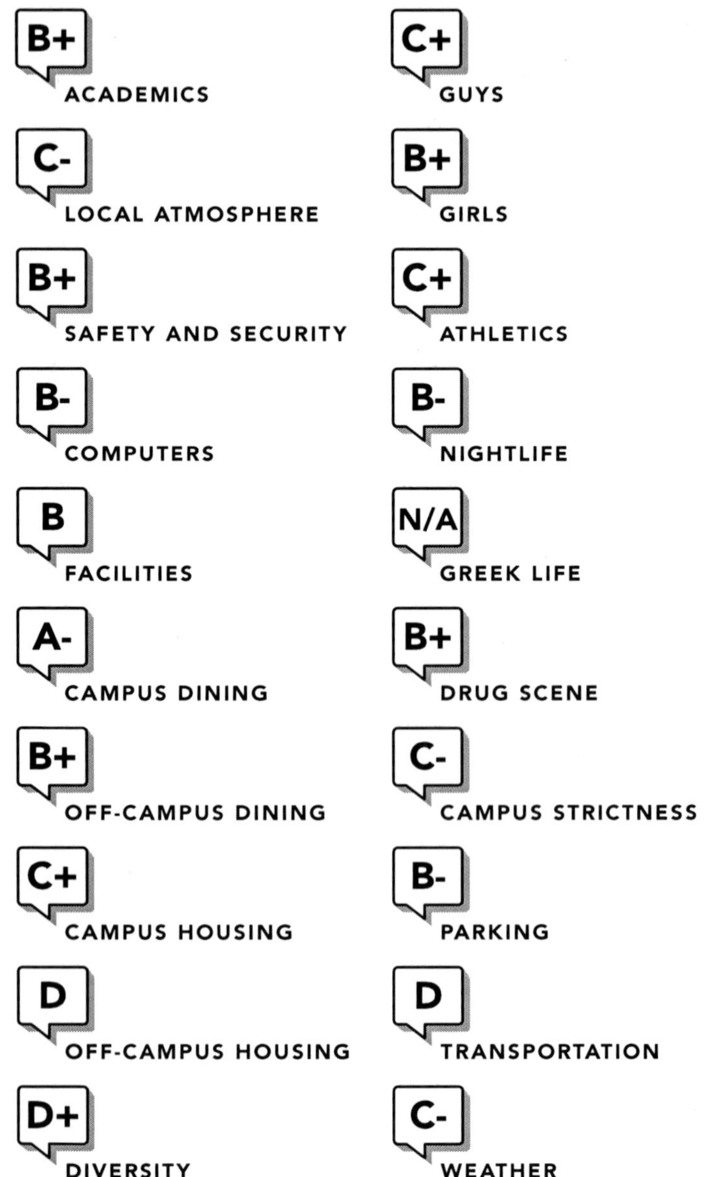

Overall Experience

Students Speak Out On...
Overall Experience

> **"I have never had any regrets about going to Colby. The time has gone too fast, and as I begin my senior year, I only wish I could do it all over again."**

Q "I love it!"

Q **"Overall my experience has been pretty good.** Different from where I came from, which I guess is what I was looking for. Yeah, I wish I was somewhere else (don't we all?), but I don't know where yet, so I'll just stay here for now."

Q **"I love this place.** If I could go back now (June 2nd) I would. The more colleges I visit my friends at, the happier I am with my choice!"

Q "I absolutely adore being at Colby. Even though it's an hour and a half to the nearest airport. The faculty is great, the people are nice and friendly, and the school does its best to take care of us and give us the best education that it can."

Q "I really like the campus, the facilities and the professors. I just wish that the campus was in California because it's so cold, so very cold."

Q "My overall experience has been great. I'm glad I traveled this far to attend college. I do not wish I were anywhere else—the environment is a great place to study and be. The people are wonderful and helpful."

Q "I wouldn't change schools for anything. I'm very happy with my choice. I came out from San Francisco looking for a new experience and I found one, and I love all the friends I've made at Colby."

Q "I love it at Colby. It seems like everyone is just so happy to be there and loves this school as much as I do. Everyone is always looking for fun things to do and more cool people to meet. The people at this school are what make it so amazing. They are down-to-earth, and love what they're doing."

Q "Colby academically far surpasses all of my expectations. Classes are great, teachers are amazing, and the workload, although heavy, is manageable if you forgo sleep, but socially, Colby seems to be drastically stunted. Life at Colby tends to revolve (like many other colleges) around alcohol. School events without alcohol are generally poorly attended, alcohol-free parties are generally abandoned early in the night in favor of alcoholic ones, and the only mass movement that the entire campus seemed to participate in was the 'Take Back Doghead' riot that incurred thousands of dollars worth of property damage."

Q "I have had a great overall experience at Colby so far. I have made some great friends, **I love my professors and classes**, and there is such a great balance between work and fun."

Q "I came to Colby because the people here are second to none. When I came to visit during the spring of my high school senior year I was overwhelmed by how incredibly welcoming and kind everyone was. Thanks to my overnight host I met so many different kinds of people, and they were all awesome. This year I reconnected with a few of the people I spent a lot of time with on that visit and we became friends. When I was here my host had someone taking me around every minute, and they were all eager to help, funny, nice, easy-going and wonderful. **I fell in love with the school before I left** the next day, and I still am in love."

Q "**I do, in fact, love Colby**. That doesn't mean that there aren't things about this school that I would like to see changed. One thing I wish was different about Colby is the prevailing sense of apathy that seems to plague the entire population."

Q "I absolutely adore Colby, and I wouldn't want to be anywhere else. **The people are great and the campus has the friendliest atmosphere**. I can't imagine what I would do without the friends I have made, and the excellent education I'm receiving."

Colby students love Colby. While they can always find something to complain about—the weather, the town, the lack of diversity, and the homework—they tend to be happy that they chose to come here. Most cite the academics and the friendly atmosphere. Classes and professors are undeniably wonderful, and the student body tends to be happy, friendly, and optimistic.

There are definitely things about Colby that should change. The school is not for everyone. The diversity issue is pretty serious, and causes the most friction on campus. Being up on Mayflower Hill all the time can drive you crazy if you can't find a way to get into town every now and then. And even when you can get into town, unless you're eating or seeing movies there's not much to do. The near-constant drinking can overwhelm some people. And the school really needs to work on a system of underground tunnels so we don't have to walk around outside in the winter. The campus, though, is bolstered by the student body's seemingly endless stores of energy and optimism, and most people have a positive Colby experience.

The Inside Scoop

Colby Slang

Know the slang, know the school. The following is a list of things you really need to know before coming to Colby. The more of these words you know, the better off you'll be.

Bob's: Short for Robert's Union, this building houses Bob's dining hall, the campus bookstore, the student newspaper offices and the campus radio station.

The Echo: The student newspaper

Frat Row: The row of small dorms lining the walkway between the library and Bob's. They used to be fraternities.

The Street: A big hallway underneath Miller Library. It's full of couches to study (or nap) on, is open twenty-four hours, and is always heated, making it a nice way to avoid the cold in the winter.

The Spa: You can't get your nails done at the Spa. It's the only non-dining hall food on campus. It's open when the dining halls aren't, and has good food that you actually have to pay for.

The Pub: Technically called the Blue Light Pub. It's what it sounds like, an on-campus pub open only to students over twenty-one.

→

Cotter: The student center, Cotter Union.

The Fishbowl: A study area in Cotter Union.

SPB: Student Programming Board. They plan things like concerts, lectures, and dances.

SGA: Student Government Association

Bro: Colby's president William "Bro" Adams. Even he calls himself Bro.

HRs: Head Residents. They keep the dorms running smoothly.

COOT: Colby Outdoor Orientation Trip. Before starting classes freshmen are thrown into the Maine wilderness for a little less than a week.

The Co-op: The first floor rooms of Mary Low. They have a kitchen and a 100 meal per semester meal plan.

Jan-plan: January. This is the time of year when you have class for eight hours a week and drink or ski the rest of the time.

Beer die: Colby's own drinking game. It involves stolen tables, dice, and plastic cups.

Beirut: The second most popular drinking game. It's a lot like beer die, except with ping-pong balls instead of dice.

The Digest: This refers both to the Digest of General Announcements, and the Digest of Civil Discourse. These are emails Colby students get every day. On the Digest of General Announcements students can post information about upcoming events, lost and found items, rides needed, etc. The Digest of Civil Discourse is a place where people can bring up things that bother them and argue a lot.

Buck Fates: A clever play on words. Colby's biggest rivalry is with Bates College in (sort of) nearby Lewiston.

The Hill: Mayflower Hill, where Colby is located.

MuleMatch: Online dating service. Wesleyan, Williams, Bowdoin, and Oberlin are also connected to this network. It's not actually used for dating, but it's a wonderful procrastination tool.

Things I Wish I Knew Before Coming to Colby

- Waterville is not a typical college town, and it's not too close to campus

- Speaking of not too close to campus, the airport's an hour and a half away

- It's totally not weird to talk to random people in the first week of classes—in fact that's how you'll make the most new and lasting friendships

- Freshmen get to have cars on campus

- Two things that could be potentially nerdy and aren't: pearls and chem.-free living

- The work will be hard, but the parties will be hard, too

Tips to Succeed at Colby

- Don't be afraid of the upperclassmen—they're your most valuable resource.

- Don't be afraid of the professors—they're good resources, too.

- Go to office hours or after class study sessions.

- Read the Digest. Or at least skim it.

- Wear your collar up

- Don't puke in your first month

- Work hard, play hard

Colby Urban Legends

There is a blue light on top of Miller Library. According to Colby myth, the light will only go out when a virgin graduates.

Secret fraternities—maybe they exist and maybe they don't.

School Spirit

While varsity sports might not be huge, Colby spirit is alive and well. Some people are apathetic, but rivalries with Bates and Bowdoin, as well as common feelings about Bro, can incite even the least spirited students to bouts of chanting. Many students feel that Colby's traditions, especially the Doghead St. Patrick's Day party, and the last day of class events, are being eliminated. These perceived injustices have led to some of the biggest displays of school spirit all year. Pretty much every car has a Colby sticker on it, and athletes love to wear their Colby gear. Students are proud of beer die, and take offense when insults are leveled at the school. A recent article in Yale's newspaper describing Colby students as immature lushes prompted immediate outcry. The school spirit at Colby is not overwhelming or football-driven, but it is definitely present and palpable.

Traditions

The Miller Steps

The steps leading to Miller Library are a symbolic beginning and end to life at Colby. One of the first things new students do, after dumping all their stuff into their dorm rooms, and meeting their roommate, is go to the steps with their parents to listen to a welcome to Colby speech. Commencement ceremonies also take place on the steps.

Champaign Toast

On the last day of classes, seniors gather on the Miller Steps (surprise, surprise) to toast the school. This sounds like a perfectly respectable and mature thing to do, until you realize that the seniors aren't toasting with glasses, they're toasting with multiple bottles. Waterville's liquor stores actually sell out of champagne in the days before the toast—many students end up going to stores in Augusta. In the past, this toast has been followed by a swim across Johnson Pond, but this was forbidden two years ago.

Doghead

Doghead is a huge party that takes place the weekend closest to St. Patrick's Day. It's usually held at an off-campus house, and people wake up as early as 4 a.m. to start drinking. This year the police heard in advance about the party, and it ended up being cancelled, but the party just ended up moving on campus. Everyone still started drinking before breakfast and partied all weekend.

Mr. Colby

This is an amazingly well attended beauty pageant featuring men rather than women. Mr. Colby is a great opportunity for the men of Colby to show of all their assets (especially their senses of humor.) Runners-up are crowned Mr. Bates and Mr. Bowdoin.

Cafeteria Tray Sledding

Colby is situated on a big hill in the middle of Maine; so obviously sledding is popular here. While people can get pretty creative about coming up with things to sled on, your college experience isn't complete until you've stolen a cafeteria tray and slid down Chapel Hill. Be careful—trays go really, really fast.

Loudness

The first and last weekend of each semester are called Loudness weekends. Bands perform and activities are planned. The first Loudness is especially great, because classes are just starting, and no one is too bogged down in homework yet. The end-of-semester Loudnesses typically feature stress-busting activities to help people get through finals.

Finding a Job or Internship

The Lowdown On...
Finding a Job or Internship

Career Services can help you with everything from finding a summer job to finding a career after college. We have no pre-med, pre-law or business majors, but if you're looking into a future in those fields, career services tends to be very helpful. There's an extensive career services library with lots of books about lots of subjects, and the counselors and faculty tend to be more than willing to talk to the students. While they have services for freshmen and sophomores, they do tend to cater to the upperclassmen a bit more.

Advice

eRecruiting is a great tool for finding a job or internship, especially for summer jobs. Even if it can't help you find the perfect employment, it can at least give you some fresh new ideas. Start getting into the career services offices as a freshman. They'll send a few emails and things, but as a youngster they won't pursue you too actively. Go to resume writing and interviewing workshops, because they're ridiculously helpful.

Career Center Resources & Services

- eRecruiting with Experience eRecuiting Network

- Vault.com

- eChoices

- Fellowship directory

- Alumni directory

- Career Counseling

Alumni

The Lowdown On...
Alumni

Website:
www.colby.edu/alumni

Office:
Office of Alumni Relations
4310 Mayflower Hill
Waterville, ME 04901
alumni@colby.edu
(207) 872-3190

Services Available
E-mail forwarding

Alumni wedding receptions at Lorimer Chapel, Millet Alumni House and Page Commons

Library use

Athletic center use (small fee)

Alumni directory

Transcript services

Major Alumni Events

Family homecoming in the fall, and reunion weekend in the summer, draw the most alumni back to Colby.

Alumni Publications

The Colby Magazine is free to current students and alums. It is published four times a year, and is available online at www.colby.edu/colby.mag

Did You Know?

Famous Colby Alumn

Doris Kearns Goodwin (Class of '64), Pulitzer Prize winning author/historian

Annie Proulx (Class of '57), Winner of the National Book Award and the Pulitzer Prize, author of The Shipping News

Billy Bush (Class of '94), Host of Access Hollywood

Student Organizations

STUDENT ORGANIZATIONS

Admissions Volunteers

Amnesty International - www.colby.edu/amnesty

Asian-American Student Association (ASA)

Asian Cultural Society

Best Buddies - www.colby.edu/bestbuddies

Biology Club (Raging Species)

The Blue Guitar

Blue Lights - www.colby.edu/blue.lights

B'nai B'rith Hillel – www.colby.edu/hillel

Broadway Musical Revue

The Bridge - www.colby.edu/bridge

Catholic Newman Council – www.colby.edu/newman.council

Chemistry Club

The C.I.R.C.L.E. (The Collective for Insight, Refuge, and the Celebration of Life Experience) – www.colby.edu/circle

Circle of Hip-Hop Culture

Class Representatives

Colby Cares About Kids (CCAK) -- www.colby.edu/ccak

Colby Cheer Club

Colby Chorale - www.colby.edu/music/perf_groups

Colby Christian Fellowship (CCF) – www.colby.edu/ccf

Colby Dancers

Colby Democrats - www.colby.edu//democrats

Colby Dinner Theatre

The Colby Echo -- www.colby.edu/echo

Colby Eight – www.colby.edu/colby-8

Colby Emergency Response (CER) -- www.colby.edu/cer

Colbyettes – www.colby.edu/colbyettes

Colby Film Society – www.colby.edu/film

Colby Handbell Choir

Colby Improv – www.colby.edu/improv

Colby Jazz Band -- www.colby.edu/jazz.band

Colby Mountaineering Club (CMC) – www.colby.edu/cmc

Colby Muslim Group – www.colby.edu/muslim

Colby Outing Club (COC) – www.colby.edu/coc

Colby Outdoor Orientation Trips (COOT) Committee – www.colby.edu/coot

Colby Republicans – www.colby.edu/republicans

Colby Sounds of Gospel

Colby South End Coalition

Colby Symphony Orchestra - www.colby.edu/music.perf_groups

Colby Volunteer Center (CVC) - www.colby.edu/cvc

Colby Wind Ensemble - www.colby.edu/music.perf_groups

Collegium Musicum - www.colby.edu/music.perf_groups

Computer Club

Cooking Club

Debate Team

Desi Club (South Asian Club)

The Difference

Economics Club

Ethnic Vocal Ensemble (EVE)

Environmental Coalition (EC) -- www.colby.edu/env.council

Environmental Education

Filipino Club

Fly Fishing Club

Four Winds

Freethinkers

French Language Club

Gathering in Christ Together – www.colby.edu/gct

Geology Club

German Language Club

Habitat for Humanity

International Club -- www.colby.edu/international

Italian Language Club

Judicial Board

Leadership Education and Advisory Program

League of Progressive Voters

Martial Arts Club – www.colby.edu/martialarts

Massage Club

Megalomaniacs – www.colby.edu/megalomaniacs

Men Against Sexism and Homophobia (MASH)

Movement for Global Justic

Musician Alliance - www.colby.edu/ma

New Moon Rising

Off-Campus Society

Powder and Wig - www.colby.edu/powderandwig

Project Ally - www.colby.edu/project_ally

Psychology Club – www.colby.edu/psych.club

Oracle

Pequod

Philosophy Club

Photography Club – www.colby.edu/photoclub

Pottery Club

Pugh Community Board

Quilting Club - www.colby.edu/quilting

Rotaract Club - www.colby.edu/rotaract

S.C.R.U.B.S. (Students at Colby Reaching to Undergraduate Biomedical Students)

SGA Films

Sirens – www.colby.edu/sirens

Skateboard Club

Society Organized Against Racism (SOAR) -- www.colby.edu/soar

Spanish Language Club

Speech Council

Student Alumni Association

Student Arts Committee

Student Government Association and President's Council – www.colby.edu/sga

Student Health On Campus (SHOC)

Student Organization for Black and Hispanic Unity (SOBHU)

Student Programming Board – www.colby.edu/spb

Student Women in Science

United World at Colby

W.A.R.M. (West and Rocky Mountains)

White Mules Pep Band

Women's Group

WMHB 89.7 FM -- www.colby.edu/wmhb

The Ten BEST Things About Colby:

1. The professors are great

2. Everyone's friendly

3. There's something to do every weekend

4. It's really easy to get involved

5. Nine out of ten people are hot

6. Security is easy-going

7. Administration gives loads of money for clubs and travel abroad

8. The campus is gorgeous

9. Differing opinions are respected, if debated ad nauseum

10. Liquor flows like water on the weekends

The Ten **WORST** Things About Colby:

1. Weather, weather, weather

2. When SPB falls through it's completely dead on campus

3. Cheap beer

4. The Jitney

5. Music at dances and concerts

6. No cities to be found

7. Small size leads to repeat hookups and a vast rumor mill

8. Student apathy

9. Cliques and status symbols

10. Liquor flows like water on the weekends

Visiting Colby

**The Lowdown On...
Visiting Colby**

Hotel Information

Among the Lakes Bed and Breakfast

www.amongthelakes.com

RR #2 Box 1075

Belgrade, ME 04917

(207) 465-4900

Distance from Campus: eight miles

Price Range: $110-$135

Best Western Waterville Inn

www.reservetravel.com

356 Main Street

Waterville, ME 04901

(207) 873-3335, (800) 528-1234

Distance from campus: 2 miles

Price Range: $95-$120

Budget Host Airport Inn

www.visitwaterville.com

400 Kennedy Memorial Drive

Waterville, ME 04901

(207) 873-3366, (800) 876-2463

Distance from campus: 2 miles

Price Range: $30-$100

Copper Heron Bed and Breakfast

www.copperheron.com

130 Main Street

Waterville, ME 04901

(207) 948-9003

Distance from campus: 1.5 miles

Price Range: $70-$80

Econo Lodge

www.watervillehamptoninn.com

425 Kennedy Memorial Drive

Waterville, ME 04901

(207) 873-0400, (800) 426-7866

Distance from campus: 2 miles

Price Range: $110-$130

Holiday Inn

www.ichotelsgroup.com

375 Upper Main Street

Waterville, ME 04901

(207) 426-7866, (800) 785-0111

Distance from campus: 2.5 miles

Price Range: $90-$110

Kozy Cove Cottages

www.kozycovecottages.com

Route 8

North Belgrade, ME 04917

(207) 465-0959

Distance from campus: 8 miles

Price Range: $550 per week

Pressey House Bed and Breakfast

www.presseyhouse.com

32 Belgrade Road

Oakland, ME 04963

(207) 463-3500

Distance from campus: 4.75 miles

Price Range: $100-$150

The Village Inn

www.villageinnducks.com

Route 27

Belgrade Lakes, ME 04918

(207) 495-3553

Distance from campus: 15 miles

Price Range: $100-$200

Whisperwood Lodge and Cottages

www.whisperwoodlodge.com

103 Taylor Woods Road

Belgrade, ME 04917

(207) 465-3983

Distance from campus: 10 miles

Price Range: $80-$150

Wings Hill Inn

www.wingshillinn.com

Route 27

Belgrade Lakes, ME 04918

(207) 495-2400

Distance from campus: 10 miles

Price Range: $100-$200

Take a Campus Virtual Tour

www.colby.edu/tour

Campus Tours

Student-led campus tours run year-round on weekdays at 9:30 a.m., 11:30 a.m., 1:30 p.m., and 3:30 p.m. They are available on Saturdays at 11 a.m. between April 1 and April 30, and between June 1 and August 31. Between September 1 and January 17 Saturday tours are available at 9:00 a.m., 11 a.m., and 12 p.m. No appointments are needed for tours, but it's a good idea to call ahead and confirm times. (207) 872-3168.

To Schedule a Group Information Session or Interview

Group Information Sessions are held weekdays, year-round, at 10:45 a.m. and 2:45 a.m. No appointments are necessary for weekday information sessions. After Labor Day, Saturday information sessions are held at 10:15 a.m. and Saturdays in April sessions are held at 10 a.m. Interviews are not required, but are strongly recommended; call (207) 872-3168 or (800) 723-3032 to schedule appointments. Off-campus interviews are available during the spring and fall.

Directions to Campus

Driving from the North

•Take Interstate 95 South to the Maine 104 exit towards Waterville/Winslow (exit 34)

•Exit to the left and stay on Main St. until the second set of lights

•Turn right onto the Eustis Parkway

•Eustis Parkway ends; turn right onto North Street (the Mid-Maine Medical Center will be on your right)

•Proceed up North Street – veer left after passing under the railroad trestle to get to the admissions office (it will be the white house on the left)

Driving from the South

•Take Interstate 95 North to Exit 127 (Waterville/Oakland)

•Turn right off the exit ramp

•Turn left at the first light (Dexter Shoe Outlet and McDonald's are on the corner)

•Follow this road past the white dormitories to a fork in the road

•Take the right fork, stay on the right after passing the athletic center

•The admissions office is a white house on the left

Words to Know

Academic Probation – A student can receive this if they fail to keep up with their school's academic minimums. Those who are unable to improve their grades after receiving this warning can possibly face dismissal.

Beer Pong / Beirut – A drinking game with numerous cups of beer arranged in a particular pattern on each side of a table. The goal is to get a ping pong ball into one of the opponent's cups by throwing the ball or hitting it with a paddle. If the ball lands in a cup, the opponent is required to drink the beer.

Bid – An invitation from a fraternity or sorority to pledge their specific house.

Blue-Light Phone – Brightly-colored phone posts with a blue light bulb on top. These phones exist for security purposes and are located at various outside locations around most campuses. If a student has an emergency or is feeling endangered, they can pick up one of these phones (free of charge) to connect with campus police or an escort service.

Campus Police – Policemen who are specifically assigned to a given institution. Campus police are not regular city officers; they are employed by the university in a full-time capacity.

Club Sports – A level of sports that falls somewhere between varsity and intramural. If a student is unable to commit to a varsity team but has a lot of passion for athletics, a club sport could be a better, less intense option. If a club sport still requires too much commitment, intramurals often involve no traveling and a lot less time.

Cocaine – An illegal drug. Also known as "coke" or "blow," cocaine often resembles a white crystalline or powdery substance. It is highly addictive and dangerous.

Common Application – An application that students can use to apply to multiple schools.

Course Registration – The time when a student selects what courses they would like for the upcoming quarter or semester. Prior to registration, it is best to have an idea of several back-up courses in case a particular class becomes full. If a course is full, a student can place themselves on the waitlist, although this still does not guarantee entry.

Division Athletics – Athletics range from Division I to Division III. Division IA is the most competitive, while Division III is considered to be the least competitive.

Dorm – Short for dormitory, a dorm is an on-campus housing facility. Dorms can provide a range of options from suite-style rooms to more communal options that include shared bathrooms. Most first-year students live in dorms. Some upperclassmen who wish to stay on campus also choose this option.

Early Action – A way to apply to a school and get an early acceptance response without a binding commitment. This is a system that is becoming less and less available.

Early Decision – An option that students should use only if they are positive that a place is their dream school. If a student applies to a school using the early decision option and is admitted, they are required and bound to attend that university. Admission rates are usually higher with early decision students because the school knows that a student is making them their first choice.

Ecstasy – An illegal drug. Also known as "E" or "X," ecstasy looks like a pill and most resembles an aspirin. Considered a party drug, ecstasy is very dangerous and can be deadly.

     Colby College **WORDS TO KNOW** | 133

Ethernet – An extremely fast internet connection that is usually available in most university-owned residence halls. To use an Ethernet connection properly, a student will need a network card and cable for their computer.

Fake ID – A counterfeit identification card that contains false information. Most commonly, students get fake IDs and change their birthdates so that they appear to be older than 21 (of legal drinking age). Even though it is illegal, many college students have fake IDs in hopes of purchasing alcohol or getting into bars.

Frosh – Slang for "freshmen."

Hazing – Initiation rituals that must be completed for membership into some fraternities or sororities. Numerous universities have outlawed hazing due to its degrading or dangerous requirements.

Sports (IMs) – A popular, and usually free, student activity where students create teams and compete against other groups for fun. These sports vary in competitiveness and can include a range of activities—everything from billiards to water polo. IM sports are a great way to meet people with similar interests.

Keg – Officially called a half barrel, a keg contains roughly 200 12-ounce servings of beer and is often found at college parties.

LSD – An illegal drug. Also known as acid, this hallucinogenic drug most commonly resembles a tab of paper.

Marijuana – An illegal drug. Also known as weed or pot; besides alcohol, marijuana is one of the most commonly-found drugs on campuses across the country.

Major –The focal point of a student's college studies; a specific topic that is studied for a degree. Examples of majors include physics, English, history, computer science, economics, business, and music. Many students decide on a specific major before arriving on campus, while others are simply "undecided" and figure it out later. Those who are extremely interested in two areas can also choose to double major.

Meal Block – The equivalent of one meal. Students on a "meal plan" usually receive a fixed number of meals per week.

Each meal, or "block," can be redeemed at the school's dining facilities in place of cash. More often than not, if a student fails to use their weekly allotment of meal blocks, they will be forfeited.

Minor – An additional focal point in a student's education. Often serving as a compliment or addition to a student's main area of focus, a minor has fewer requirements and prerequisites to fulfill than a major. Minors are not required for graduation from most schools; however some students who want to further explore many different interests choose to have both a major and a minor.

Mushrooms – An illegal drug. Also known as "shrooms," this drug looks like regular mushrooms but are extremely hallucinogenic.

Off-Campus Housing – Housing from a particular landlord or rental group that is not affiliated with the university. Depending on the college, off-campus housing can range from extremely popular to non-existent. Those students who choose to live off campus are typically given more freedom, but they also have to deal with things such as possible subletting scenarios, furniture, and bills. In addition to these factors, rental prices and distance often affect a student's decision to move off campus.

Office Hours – Time that teachers set aside for students who have questions about the coursework. Office hours are a good place for students to go over any problems and to show interest in the subject material.

Pledging – The time after a student has gone through rush, received a bid, and has chosen a particular fraternity or sorority they would like to join. Pledging usually lasts anywhere from one to two semesters. Once the pledging period is complete and a particular student has done everything that is required to become a member, they are considered a brother or sister. If a fraternity or a sorority would decide to "haze" a group of students, these initiation rituals would take place during the pledging period.

Private Institution – A school that does not use taxpayers dollars to help subsidize education costs. Private schools typically cost more than public schools and are usually smaller.

Prof – Slang for "professor."

Public Institution – A school that uses taxpayers dollars to help subsidize education costs. Public schools are often a good value for in-state residents and tend to be larger than most private colleges.

Quarter System (sometimes referred to as the Trimester System) – A type of academic calendar system. In this setup, students take classes for three academic periods. The first quarter usually starts in late September or early October and concludes right before Christmas. The second quarter usually starts around early to mid–January and finishes up around March or April. The last quarter, or "third quarter," usually starts in late March or early April and finishes up in late May or Mid-June. The fourth quarter is summer. The major difference between the quarter system and semester system is that students take more courses but with less coverage.

RA (Resident Assistant) – A student leader who is assigned to a particular floor in a dormitory in order to help to the other students who live there. A RA's duties include ensuring student safety and providing guidance or assistance wherever possible.

Recitation – An extension of a specific course; a "review" session of sorts. Because some classes are so large, recitations offer a setting with fewer students where students can ask questions and get help from professors or TAs in a more personalized environment. As a result, it is common for most large lecture classes to be supplemented with recitations.

Rolling Admissions – A form of admissions. Most commonly found at public institutions, schools with this type of policy continue to accept students throughout the year until their class sizes are met. For example, some schools begin accepting students as early as December and will continue to do so until April or May.

Room and Board – This is typically the combined cost of a university-owned room and a meal plan.

Room Draw/Housing Lottery – A common way to pick on-campus room assignments for the following year. If a student decides to remain in university-owned housing, they are assigned a unique number that, along with seniority, is used to choose their new rooms for the next year.

Rush – The period in which students can meet the brothers and sisters of a particular chapter and find out if a given fraternity or sorority is right for them. Rushing a fraternity or a sorority is not a requirement at any school. The goal of rush is to give students who are serious about pledging a feel for what to expect.

Semester System – The most common type of academic calendar system at college campuses. This setup typically includes two semesters in a given school year. The "fall" semester starts around the end of August or early September and finishes right before winter vacation. The "spring" semester usually starts in mid-January and ends around late April or May.

Student Center/Rec Center/Student Union – A common area on campus that often contains study areas, recreation facilities, and eateries. This building is often a good place to meet up with fellow students and is most commonly used as a hangout. Depending on the school, the student center can have a huge role or a non-existent role in campus life.

Student ID – A university-issued photo ID that serves as a student's key to many different functions within an institution. Some schools require students to show these cards in order to get into dorms, libraries, cafeterias, and other facilities. In addition to storing meal plan information, in some cases, a student ID can actually work as a debit card and allow students to purchase things from bookstores or local shops.

Suite – A type of dorm room. Unlike other places that have communal bathrooms that are shared by the entire floor, a suite has a private bathroom. Suite-style dorm rooms can house anywhere from two to ten students.

TA (Teacher's Assistant) – An undergraduate or grad student who helps in some manner with a specific course. In some cases, a TA will teach a class, assist a professor, grade assignments, or conduct office hours.

Undergraduate – A student who is in the process of studying for their Bachelor (college) degree.

ABOUT THE AUTHOR:

Hi! I'm the author. While not writing college guidebooks, I actually go to college. I'm currently a sophomore at Colby. I think I'm an English major, but that's subject to change on a minute-by-minute basis. I'm also a political junkie. At school I'm the Arts and Entertainment editor for the Echo, the president of the League of Progressive Voters (like I said, political junkie), an HR and a tour guide.

I have lived in northern Virginia, the western suburbs of Chicago, and now Maine.

I think writing is fun, and I think writing about myself is disconcerting. So I'm going to stop and thank some people very quickly.

Thanks to my family, especially my parents. Thanks to my friends, who I will not list by name because I would probably forget somebody or put someone last and I don't want to do that. Thanks to the College Prowler. Thanks to my teachers. Thanks to you, dear reader, for putting up with my writing.

Good luck with the college search. If you have any comments about the guidebook or questions about Colby, the application process, the meaning of life, etc., I enjoy receiving emails. They make me feel loved.

Allyson Rudolph

allysonrudolph@collegeprowler.com

Notes

Notes

Notes

Notes

Notes

Notes

Notes

Notes

Notes

Notes

Notes

Notes

Notes

Notes

Notes

Notes

Notes

Notes

Need More Help?

Do you have more questions about this school? Can't find a certain statistic? College Prowler is here to help. We are the best source of college information on the planet. We have a network of thousands of students who can get the latest information on any school to you ASAP. E-mail us at *info@collegeprowler.com* with your college-related questions. It's like having an older sibling show you the ropes!

Email Us Your College-Related Questions!

Check out **www.collegeprowler.com** for more details.
1.800.290.2682

Notes

Tell Us What Life Is Really Like At Your School!

Have you ever wanted to let people know what your school is really like? Now's your chance to help millions of high school students choose the right school.

Let your voice be heard and win cash and prizes!

Check out **www.collegeprowler.com** for more info!

Notes

Do You Have What It Takes To Get Admitted?

The College Prowler Road to College Counseling Program is here. An admissions officer will review your candidacy at the school of your choice and create a 12+ page personal admission plan. We rate your credentials with the same criteria used by school admissions committees. We assess your strengths and weaknesses and create a plan of action that makes a difference.

Check out **www.collegeprowler.com** or call 1.800.290.2682 for complete details.

Notes

Pros and Cons

Still can't figure out if this is the right school for you? You've already read through this in-depth guide; why not list the pros and cons? It will really help with narrowing down your decision and determining whether or not this school is right for you.

Pros	Cons

Notes

Need Help Paying For School?

Apply for our Scholarship!

College Prowler awards thousands of dollars a year to students who compose the best essays. E-mail *scholarship@collegeprowler.com* for more information, or call 1.800.290.2682.

Apply now at **www.collegeprowler.com**

Notes

Get Paid To Rep Your City!

Make money for college!

Earn cash by telling your friends about College Prowler!

Excellent Pay + Incentives + Bonuses

Compete with reps across the nation for cash bonuses

Gain marketing and communication skills

Build your resume and gain work experience for future career opportunities

Flexible work hours; make your own schedule

Opportunities for advancement

Contact *sales@collegeprowler.com*
Apply now at **www.collegeprowler.com**

Notes

Do You Own A Website?

Would you like to be an affiliate of one of the fastest-growing companies in the publishing industry? Our web affiliates generate a significant income based on customers whom they refer to our website. Start making some cash now! Contact *sales@collegeprowler.com* for more information or call 1.800.290.2682

Apply now at **www.collegeprowler.com**

Notes

Reach A Market Of Over 24 Million People.

Advertising with College Prowler will provide you with an environment in which your message will be read and respected. Place your message in a College Prowler guidebook, and let us start bringing long-lasting customers to you. We deliver high-quality ads in color or black-and-white throughout our guidebooks.

Contact Joey Rahimi
joey@collegeprowler.com
412.697.1391
1.800.290.2682

Check out **www.collegeprowler.com** for more info.

Notes

Write For Us!

Get Published! Voice Your Opinion.

Writing a College Prowler guidebook is both fun and rewarding; our open-ended format allows your own creativity free reign. Our writers have been featured in national newspapers and have seen their names in bookstores across the country. Now is your chance to break into the publishing industry with one of the country's fastest-growing publishers!

Apply now at **www.collegeprowler.com**

Contact *editor@collegeprowler.com* or
call 1.800.290.2682 for more details.

Notes

Do You Own A Website?

Would you like to be an affiliate of one of the fastest-growing companies in the publishing industry? Our web affiliates generate a significant income based on customers whom they refer to our website. Start making some cash now! Contact *sales@collegeprowler.com* for more information or call 1.800.290.2682

Apply now at **www.collegeprowler.com**

Notes

Reach A Market Of Over 24 Million People.

Advertising with College Prowler will provide you with an environment in which your message will be read and respected. Place your message in a College Prowler guidebook, and let us start bringing long-lasting customers to you. We deliver high-quality ads in color or black-and-white throughout our guidebooks.

Contact Joey Rahimi
joey@collegeprowler.com
412.697.1391
1.800.290.2682

Check out **www.collegeprowler.com** for more info.

Notes

Write For Us!

Get Published! Voice Your Opinion.

Writing a College Prowler guidebook is both fun and rewarding; our open-ended format allows your own creativity free reign. Our writers have been featured in national newspapers and have seen their names in bookstores across the country. Now is your chance to break into the publishing industry with one of the country's fastest-growing publishers!

Apply now at **www.collegeprowler.com**

Contact *editor@collegeprowler.com* or call 1.800.290.2682 for more details.

Notes